MICHAEL BOYD

# An Ordinary MAN

*The memoirs of an ordinary man who
enjoyed the occasional moment of success*

MICHAEL BOYD

# An Ordinary MAN

**MEMOIRS**
Cirencester

Published by Memoirs

MEMOIRS
PUBLISHING

1A The Market Place Cirencester Gloucestershire GL7 2PR
info@memoirsbooks.co.uk | www.memoirspublishing.com

**An Ordinary Man**

ISBN: 978-1-86151-109-6

# Contents

Introduction

Dedication

Acknowledgements

# Introduction

My life has been ordinary, in common with millions of people of my time and millions more who came before. Nevertheless in writing the memoirs of my life I have gained much personal pleasure. There is pain, there are tears too, but there is also laughter in abundance.

These recollections are mostly individual to me, but of course they embrace my entire family as well as the many thousands of people I have met through school, work and life. There are close-ups, angry exchanges, childhood wonderment, life-threatening moments, delight, despair and pure pleasure. The storyline does not always go the way I wanted it to, but then life rarely lets you write your own script.

This book has taken a couple of years to write. It begins with my earliest recollections of a simple country childhood and continues through a hectic business career to my pensionable years. I have endeavoured throughout to maintain a positive slant wherever possible, just occasionally being less than charitable about the odd individual. Events have been recounted as I have recalled them in the sequence they hit the keyboard, with each leading on to a new one, sometimes detailed, sometimes sketchy.

I have recorded in detail many events of my working life over 39 years. These accounts may not always make for easy understanding, but I was passionate about my job and each achievement gave me great satisfaction, in what was always a challenging environment. I hope the account of my working years gives a hint of my own unique style as well as my determination and desire to succeed.

These chapters will reveal my intolerant nature, willingness to embrace conflict and my overwhelming desire to win. As a famous American president once said, "do what you can, with what you have, where you are", and I did so, as often as I could. Writing about my now almost anonymous successes at work has been a wonderful experience.

Deep inside, this 'ordinary man' wants to be remembered down the ages, and not just as a name on a family tree or as a great-great-granddad in a photo. For me this story will I hope give colour and recognition to an ordinary man's life without the writer's ego having run amok. If you enjoy one single line, my pleasure will be immense.

This book is dedicated to my family,
all of whom have provided me with great pride,
pleasure, warmth and love.

# Acknowledgements

I would like to thank my wife Lorraine, who has spent many hours without complaint reading through my story from its earliest drafts, and Chris Newton of Memoirs Books for turning my rough manuscript form into a readable book.

October 2013

# CHAPTER ONE

# A Somerset childhood

Life begins on the 16<sup>th</sup> Jan 1947, in one of the coldest winters on record. Home is a wooden bungalow on the outskirts of the village of West Harptree in Somerset, no more than a mile from Moreton, soon to be drowned under the waters of a new reservoir, Chew Valley Lake. That bungalow is no longer standing.

I am the first child of John Boyd and Brenda Boyd (née Tucker). We are to live in this bungalow, really no more than a shack, for the first three years of my life before moving to a council house in the nearby village of Compton Martin, where my sisters Kate and Jenny are born in 1950 and 1951.

It is difficult to isolate memories of my earliest days other than a vague recollection of the births of my sisters, both born at home. I have an elder half-brother, Tony, born to my mother six years earlier, who lived his early life with my grandmother and grandfather.

I begin writing the story of my life so far the day after my 64th birthday. Life has been immensely kind and equally cruel over my 64 years and I seek to record the fullest of memories, from the earliest point of recall. I have rounded the corners a little, but I have made every effort to retain a factual account of those years so that my children and grandchildren can rekindle memories, fill in missing pieces, and, who knows, perhaps allow those I have not known to learn a little about me in years to come should they wish. It may also give them a knowledge of my relatives, so that one day the memoirs might just trigger a recognition of a relative who would otherwise never have been known. It may also give them the opportunity to recognise a place where I played, worked or lived.

At certain points along the way the rose-tinted glasses may be apparent and passages of particular enjoyment, achievement or difficulty may be extended beyond the reader's interest, in which case please forgive me. My life has been ordinary, but nonetheless special to me, and if you are reading this it might in part have been important to you, your parents or to someone down the line of ancestry. Hopefully my more pleasurable and poignant moments will be sufficiently interesting to grab your attention here and there.

Throughout my life I have always been able to recall moments from the past, some innocuous, others of importance, frequently in significant detail, and this has helped me immensely in writing these memoirs. Of course age can dull and life can add a touch of colour. As I write, so those moments are woven into the storyline, sometimes as a simple record, on other occasions as a simple fact or merely set in a time of important change. The story and recollections are not always in strict order of their occurrence, but I hope they will take you easily through my life and highlight the many memories which flowed back to me during the course of writing this.

My father was from Widnes, Lancashire (it is now in Cheshire) where many of my cousins still live. Dad had a brother James and a sister Francis. Dad's father died before Dad was born in 1916 while on leave from the First World War trenches, the cause of death being pneumonia. Dad's mum (née Kelly) passed away on the 14th June 1946 having brought up the three children on her own, so I knew neither of my grandparents on my father's side and contact with my northern relatives has been minimal over the years, holidays and funerals sadly bringing the only meetings. I have in recent months spoke to Mary and Fran, two of my cousins and daughters of my Dad's sister, about these memories, to establish some simple facts about my grandparents which had until now been unknown.

Dad met Mum when he was serving in the army at Yoxter Rifle Camp, which was between Charterhouse and Priddy near the top of the Mendips; today I believe it is a rifle range. Mum was from West Harptree and had two brothers, Gordon and Dennis, and three sisters,

Thelma, Dolly and Audrey. Mum's brothers and sisters moved not far from their origins, living at Radstock, East Harptree, Bristol and two in Weston Super Mare. I have many cousins, some of whom I don't even know. Others, Cecil, Clarence and Desmond Currell, sons of Thelma, still live I believe at East Harptree. Alan Archer, son of Audrey, lives at Weston, others in Bristol, and I have at least five cousins living in or near Widnes, most in their seventies, though young Fran, as she has always been known, is very close to my age.

My first real recollections of childhood come from when I was around four years old. Some dates I recall easily, but for the most part they are not my forte. I remember a day spent with my grandmother, whom I adored. My mum's parents lived in West Harptree in a row of houses known as Magpie Alley. Sadly all have been demolished now, but they would have been found on the right hand side of the road as you leave West Harptree to drive to Bishop Sutton.

On this day, however, something had upset me. I cannot recall, what but I know I sat outside sulking and refusing to eat, even though I was hungry. I remember being angry and determined not to eat no matter how much my grandmother tried to persuade me. I noticed how hurt my grandmother was that I would not eat. My behaviour on that day lives with me even now. When I got home I was sad for the rest of the day. I never did behave that badly again when staying with my grandmother.

At four years and three months old I was off to school at West Harptree Primary School about two and half miles away. We caught the bus there and back each day. One of the older children from the Buildings (the name of the 24-house council estate where I lived – it has since been poshly renamed Mendip Villas) looked after me briefly, namely getting on and off the bus walking into the school. It was a Church of England school and was across the road from the Crown Inn pub. The bus stopped almost directly outside the church.

Day one was eventful. At playtime a fight broke out between myself and a West Harptree lad named Jimmy Edwards, possibly a mite older than me and certainly a wee bit larger. The fight consisted of an argument, pushing and then some rough and tumble. Eventually I got him in a headlock and did not let go until the bell went for the return to class. At the 50th anniversary of Chew Valley School's opening, I bumped into Jimmy Edwards for the first time in some forty years and recollections of the scrap came bursting back. I did not remind Jimmy of the event though something about his eyes told me he remembered that school spat. Well, he stood six feet eight inches tall and with me being only five foot six it seemed sensible to let it pass. Good job he was not that tall back in 1951.

West Harptree School took in children from Compton Martin and West Harptree villages in the main. There was a Head Teacher, Miss Mclanen, and her deputy, Mrs Shutt. My parents never had a car, so we caught the bus to and from school each day. Once at school we had to walk to the village hall for our lunches, and I recall on one occasion having to eat cabbage, which I hated then and still do. The Head Teacher, whose table I was unfortunate enough to sit at on one occasion for lunch, spotted I was not eating my cabbage and told me she too disliked it. She then proceeded to sprinkle sugar over hers. "Now Boyd, try doing the same" she said. I did - it was dreadful. I always endeavoured to avoid her table thereafter and did so with total success for the short period I remained at the school.

During the winter our school milk would be heated on an old coal/coke stove. School milk was free in those days, one third of a pint on every school day, and it was a wonderful moment as we all gathered around the stove. The school had very little heating and it was a real chance to be warm inside and out. The milk really did taste so much better when it was heated.

The toilets were outside in part of the playground and the boys' urinal had no roof. During playtime girls and boys played in separate playgrounds - a mite old fashioned, but so was life at this time, not quite Victorian but only six years after World War 2 and there was real austerity. We did our PE in the playground summer and winter. The latter was often very cold and our equipment was simply a collection of bean bags, though as far as I can recall we all enjoyed it, probably because it was not a lesson.

The school however brought new disciplines; no

talking, concentration, no going to the toilet during lessons (not good in a cold school), arithmetic, spelling, reading and writing as dictated by the teacher. Teachers were strict and Mrs Shutt certainly had no warmth for me, nor was I particularly bright, though I was a little difficult and often talked when I should not have, and for this I was frequently punished. One day I was made to sit next to a girl known to constantly have fleas and told I would be sitting with her for the rest of the year. Even though I was not yet five, I saw this as a deliberate attempt to make me look silly in front of everyone. It was also very unkind to me and to the girl, who carried the cross of the fleas for all her school life. On reaching adulthood she became a prostitute. Children can be so unkind to one another and one wonders if she was ever loved.

Even though I was less than five years old, I decided that I was not going to put up with the teacher punishing me in this way. The punishment was unfair and very unkind towards the girl. So I left the school and walked home. In those days there were no playground attendants and teachers rarely came into the playground except to ring the bell for return to class. At 64 there is doubt in my mind that I really did walk home - after all it was two and half miles. Surely someone would have stopped and asked me where I was going and asked why I was not at school, although in those days traffic was very light. Down the years my recall has always been of walking out and walking home. I told my mother I would never be going back to West Harptree school again because of what Mrs. Shutt had done, and Dad could beat me all he liked but I was not going back. And I never did. I never spent another day there.

School life restarted at the Sacred Heart High School in Chew Magna. This was a private fee-paying school for girls up to the age of 18 and boys up to the age of 11. The school was run by nuns, the only exception being the PE teacher, who was Mrs Patten. She lived just up the road from us and in later years I drank occasionally with her son.

During the five and bit years that followed much was enjoyable but often embarrassing, and cemented my socialist views and beliefs. The difference between the fee-paying pupils and the Catholic paupers was constantly apparent. Our uniforms were almost invariably secondhand. My sisters attended the Sacred Heart throughout their school years, and we all knew we were of less wealthy stock and most of those attending were from well-to-do families who had plenty of money. Our entry to the school had been free, as we were Roman Catholics. The school was run by the nuns, who had dedicated their lives to worshipping and serving God. This period of my life left me forever believing in God, and that belief has never left me. On days filled with personal pain, unwanted news and inevitable events, belief provides shelter from reality.

The nuns did all the teaching and were very good,

though I was a difficult case. I got my head around maths with consummate ease, at least the basics, but English was a different ball game altogether. I found the whole issue of spelling, punctuation and even the alphabet more complex than algorithms.

During my years at the Sacred Heart, Lent was a wonderful period. A 40-day fast for Roman Catholics, it was observed by giving up luxuries such as sweets and chocolate, and all children attending the school were expected to hand over their goodies for the entire period, be they Catholic or not. Almost all of them did. There was no problem for us plebs as we hardly ever had any sweets. I recall some of the nuns with the fondest of memories as I write, such as Sister Francis, who was always so very kind to me, Sister Anthony, six feet tall, Sister Agnes, so softly spoken and Sister Munchin, who seemed always 100 years old to me as a child. They would collect all the sweets and redistribute them to the children who were at the school by favour, to be eaten at home of course out of sight of the other children. On these occasion being a poor Catholic boy was a joy and wondrous time, and not for one day but for forty days each year.

We were a poor family, not the poorest of the poor but close enough. My father was a builder's labourer and in later life a bin man (refuse collector). My mother cleaned other people's houses and had been in service as a young teenage girl. My parents were nevertheless proud people. They held very firm views on life and attended church almost every week. Both were staunch Labour supporters and our house during General Elections was used as the local Committee Rooms for the Labour Party. The council house we lived in was rather chilly, heated only by open coal fires which were often not lit until late afternoon and on most occasions only in the sitting room. It was an act of bravery on a January evening to get into bed and it was unbelievably cold. Once in the bed you simply did not move, and when you woke on a January or February morning the insides of the windows were iced over. It sounds terrible, but at the time it also seemed totally normal and all the other children in the buildings experienced the same awakening.

I cannot say we were ever left really hungry. Breakfast was always a bowl of piping hot porridge, sometimes thinner, sometimes thicker, very occasionally topped with treacle. In the absence of treacle a sprinkling of white sugar was allowed. If things were tight the porridge would be replaced with bread and milk. Lunch was the school meal, free all the time we attended the Sacred Heart. Tea was potato and vegetables and a very small portion of meat, half a sausage for instance, a piece of fatty pork, or sometimes a faggot, a real treat. Chicken was eaten only at Christmas. We had half a boiled egg and toast for Sunday tea and butter was as precious as diamonds. Bread and jam was a frequent meal. Most of the jam was homemade, nearly always plum or blackcurrant.

Much of our meat intake was offal, including chitterling - pigs' intestine, which Mum cleaned herself, buying it by the bucketful for a few pence from the butcher's (Veaters) at West Harptree. On one occasion she found a large live tapeworm, 15 to 20cms long, inside the intestine she was cleaning. It was a long while before we again had chitterling. Today I still enjoy a plate of chitterling with oceans of vinegar, salt and pepper. We also ate many stews, mostly meat bones (sometimes a couple of rabbit legs from the neighbour next door, who shot wild rabbits from the local fields (no myxomatosis when I was a boy), with vegetables from the garden. The stew included enormous "doughboys" made from fat or suet and flour rolled into large balls and cooked with the stew, very filling. The juices were always really good and though the meat left around the bones was minimal it was very succulent, so this was a much enjoyed meal.

As a young boy I cannot say that I really felt poor. My childhood was a pretty happy one. We got a single present at Christmas. My first recollection, probably again at four years of age, was going with my father on the back of a push bike (the bike had a child's seat on it) to Symes' shop in West Harptree on Christmas Day. The shop owner was quite willing to open up and let us in. Dad bought me a green tractor and even now as I write I can still sense the sheer excitement all the way home on the bike (two miles and a bit). It was my first ever new toy. In the Christmases until I was eleven I was invariably given a clockwork train set, which during the course of the year would always get broken. A cowboy gun was a frequent request for my birthday, but I was not always lucky.

By the age of about ten, I had developed a real interest in toy soldiers and badgered my mum at every chance to buy them for me. The soldiers were invariably made of metal, plastic yet to gain popularity. Thinking back now those tin soldiers must have been the beginning of my DIY traits. Forts and castles were built from strong cardboard, cut, glued and painted and imaginary wars embarked upon by the soldiers. An elastic band and finely-folded paper pellets provided the weaponry by which the wars were fought, which gave many hours of pleasure.

Looking back is of course nearly always more comfortable, for whatever may have happened you know you've got through it, so I have to be careful not to wear those rose-tinted glasses too much. Nevertheless much was good during my childhood years. I spent as much time as I was allowed with my grandmother, school holidays and weekends from about the age of six. I cannot recall however my sisters spending time with her. My half-brother Tony was six years older than me and had lived with Grand from the day he was born until he joined the Navy, and in fact until he got married, by which time only 'Granfer Dick' was alive. Grand died when I was ten but for the moment I shall share all those good and wonderful things that happen over the four years or so that I stayed with her on and off.

The house that Grand (whose maiden name was Elsie Rains) and Granfer Dick (also known as Dickie Mint) lived in was rented, and back in 1953 it had no electricity, no hot water and no inside toilet. The toilet was in the yard in a small shed and consisted of a wooden bench with a seat-shaped opening, underneath which sat a large bucket which was emptied once a week into a six-foot trench at the bottom of the garden. This trench, my grandfather told me, would be re-dug every fifteen years and moved about five feet each time. This part of the garden was farthest from the house, naturally. This trench housed not only human waste but more sinister items, for back in those days there were none of the niceties of neutered cats, and when the cats had kittens my grandfather would take them at a few days old and summarily, with a sharp flick of his wrist, thrash them across his boot and deposit them into the trench. Dreadful as this may sound, there was no cruelty, no pain. It was just the practicality of life, my grand parents could afford no other way.

There were three bedrooms, a kitchen with a flagstone floor, a dining room and a sitting room in which there was a massive range with two large ovens and a very big hob, upon which sat a black and almost constantly boiling kettle. Grand did all the cooking on this range, which was fired by coal and wood. The overall fireplace was so large that four people could sit under the chimney breast, and at night you could look up the chimney and see the stars and sky. Outside there were stables where once coal horses had been kept, but in my time they were used mainly for Granfer Dick's bicycle business, which he ran as a sideline (he put together a wonderful red bicycle with a brand new saddle for my fourteenth birthday (the first real bicycle I had ever had). His normal work was as a labourer for Bristol Waterworks.

There was also a large dirt yard and big vegetable plot. Hens and bantams were kept for eggs and meat but I cannot really remember eating any of the hens. The bantams were ferocious little blighters. There was I recall on one occasion a bantam cockerel chasing me across the yard, and Grand in order to protect me from it, took a massive swing at it with a spade and decapitated it. It continued to run without its head for another twenty metres, but fortunately for me it went straight past, unsighted you might say.

Life at Grand's was very different from home, almost Victorian, but always enjoyable. In the sitting room, the oil lamps would be lit in the evening as dark approached, and the huge range would be stoked for the evening. You went outside to the toilet just before dark and used the pot thereafter, which was kept under the bed. Grand would take me to bed using a candle to light the way, but I don't believe she left the candle in the bedroom. I do recall that the house had two sets of stairs and there was no landing, so you had to walk through the bedrooms to get to the middle one where I slept with my brother.

There were three shops in the village. One was Payne's, which is still open, though no longer called Payne's, and oddly enough my sister Jennifer has worked there for more than 20 years at the last count. The others were Diamonds and Symes', where Grand did most of her shopping. I would often go to the shops for her.

Once a week the Tizer man came, delivering lemonade and the likes. The rag and bone man also came about once a month and Grand would collect old cloths, sacks, etc and sell them to him, often for as little as a penny or two. His name was Nuttall, but everyone called him Nutty for short. The other regular caller to the house was Mr Parsley, who delivered fuels for the lamps and the gas camping burner. Grand sometimes used it to give the kettle a quick boost before making a cup of tea. Mr Parsley also sold the filaments for the lamps and the tins of paint which Granfer used to touch up his bicycles. As I grew older I bought them too. Mr Parsley also called at home, and I still remember the small Bedford truck he drove.

In the summer evenings I played tennis or football on the main road with my brother Tony, who often let me win. We stretched a piece of rope across the road to act as a net and put coats on the road for goalposts. Traffic was very light and vehicles rarely came to interrupt our evening games. It was after all the mid 1950s and relative wealth for the masses was some way off. Early mornings in late summer we would set off across the fields to go mushrooming. One particular morning after an hour of searching we found six reasonably-sized field mushrooms which my Grand turned into a marvellous breakfast. She added some real fatty bacon and eggs and we had large chunks of bread to soak up the mushroom and bacon juice. The four of us sat down to eat and Granfer Dick said on finishing his breakfast that he had enjoyed it so much that that evening I would get a lemonade stout for supper. This was a bottled Mackeson, alcoholic and wonderful with a dash of lemonade - Granfer called it medicinal. I remember that breakfast because I was the one who found the mushrooms, and all the previous days for two weeks we had not found a single one.

During the winter evenings I got to play cards with Granfer Dick but he rarely let me win. They were truly smashing times, life was good and I walked the fields with Toby, Grand's old mongrel dog, for hours. On other days we wandered across to the pond in the field opposite the house, which was always teeming with life - tadpoles, sticklebacks, leeches, water beetles and so on. I would spend much time catching the inhabitants and then returning them to the pond before heading back to Grand's. Who would not enjoy such pleasurable moments? Certainly this lad did.

\* \* \* \* \*

I remember that on the last occasion I stayed with my

Grand I was aged around nine, possibly ten, making my Grand a cup of tea, as she had been feeling unwell all day and was so pleased that I was able to make it for her. I had used a new Calor gas cooker which she had managed to save up for over many years. I recall now that it was pale green with some black mottling in the enamel paint and stood gleaming in the old kitchen against the flagstone floor. My Grand was so very proud of it, saving for many years before she could afford to buy one.

Later that same year my Grand died of cancer. I prayed for her every single night, I was so very sad. I missed my Grand, Toby, the stout shandy and the very rare lemonade and ice cream sodas. I missed occasions like the day Tony and I sailed a model boat across part of the new Chew Valley lake while the lake was being built - it took nearly all day. We simply set the boat afloat at one end and somehow or the other it sailed to the other side. In between we searched for birds' nests; my brother had a very nice collection of eggs, which he kept in a red box filled with sawdust.

Back at home we played cricket in the Buildings. If the ball was hit into someone's garden you were out, and if the house was one where they didn't give it you back, you had to sneak in and retrieve it. Sometimes if you got caught in the garden you were given a severe clip around the ear and you lost your ball. The game had to be abandoned, and sometimes it was weeks before the ball was returned - very occasionally, never.

At the age of seven I went on our first and my only holiday with my parents and sisters to Widnes, where we stayed with Dad's sister, Aunt Frances. It was for me a tremendous adventure, and the whole trip filled me with wonder. We went in a taxi to Temple Meads railway station. I had never been in a car or on a train, two big firsts for me. I can still smell the station in my nostrils even now. The sulphur from the coal that was burned to drive the steam engines of 1954 was very pungent. The station was full of people - I had never seen so many people in one place in my entire life. They were of every shape, size and attire. Many seemed in a hurry, excited children like myself making much noise, everyone carrying large and very heavy suitcases. Odd-looking three-wheeled vehicles with fat noses pulled trailers stacked with more suitcases; so much new information to take in and I wasn't even on the train yet.

Boarding the train was like entering another world. The carriages with their very upright seats made of material I had never seen and with their own unique smells intrigued me as much as did the people who sat opposite.

The journey was to last for ever, well several hours. As we passed through Box Tunnel the lights inside the train barely lit the carriage sufficiently for me to see my parents and as we travelled through the tunnel time appeared to stop, filling me full of wonderment as the light rushed back into the carriages on exiting the tunnel. The train journey seemed endless, through towns, cities and ever-changing countryside, stopping now and then at a station. Here there were more people, some getting on, some getting off, rather mundane but not to this seven-year-old. We changed trains at Crewe, I think for Runcorn, where we departed for my aunt's. It was a most pleasurable journey, and I guess for the first time I became aware of how much I enjoyed the very simple things of life. I remained enthralled throughout the long journey and never once, as I recall, asked when we would get to Widnes, only wondering endlessly what it would be like, and whether it would be like Compton Martin or West Harptree.

It turned out to be very different from the green fields of home. Even the people spoke differently. New adventures though were abundant. We travelled on the Mersey ferry and went to watch marching bands, it seemed like hundreds of them though in reality there were probably twenty or so, each in beautifully coloured uniforms, belting out Salvation Army type music and marching in perfect lines, led by a majorette whose skills with the baton mesmerized me. But the towns around Widnes seemed dull and almost threatening. The houses were grey and joined one after the other for as far as you could see and walk. Narrow alleyways abounded. There were small gardens seen only through the odd open alley door, and each showed signs of neglect. Some were heaped with rubbish and others were black, without a blade of grass.

I remember playing with the lad who lived next door

to my Aunt Frances. We went off with about 10 other lads to this waste ground, where he told me that they all liked to fight and today if I wanted to play, then I would have to fight with the rest of them. I was not very keen but agreed to fight him and anyone that was about my size. Most looked like giants to me, but they probably were not that big. In the end I must have had about six fights in total. I do not recall the fights being that rough, but he told me they did it most days and really enjoyed it. The journey home was not quite so exciting, and eight years later when the family went again I was 15 and far too old to go on holiday with them. In any case I had a girlfriend and the house was empty.

From the age of about eight, I had become an avid collector of birds' eggs. At the age of eight I was totally unaware of the 1954 Act which prohibited the collection of wild bird eggs. During my childhood, intensive farming with its high dependency on chemical control of weeds and insects had not yet arrived to cause a decline in the bird population. There was, as far as I am able to recall over the years, no real human pressure either on bird habitats. My interest in collecting eggs had been fired by my brother's collection, which he later gave to me, but from the age of around eight, I looked forward to those two key egg-collecting months, April and May, every year up to the age of fourteen. I walked mile upon mile in search of eggs, sometimes on my own, sometimes with other lads from the Buildings. We were careful not to take more than one egg from any nest. As the years progressed the collection grew ever bigger, with entire boxes of rooks and carrion crow eggs, each having their own beautiful individual markings of light green overlaid with dark greens and pencil thin black squiggles, some with a minor shade of blue, although this was a very rare marking.

As time moved on much of the bird nesting I did was with Alan Gould, who lived in the Buildings and was about three years older than me. The rooks' and crows' nests were particularly challenging as they nested in such high trees, mostly elms in those days and often in the very tips of the branches, so getting to the nest was always a bit more difficult for me, simply because I was small, and returning to the ground with an egg still intact meant climbing back down with great care. On occasions the egg would break and was not fit for display.

One day I fell the last 12 to 14 feet, hitting the ground with a thud, and looked up to see a young bird hanging from the barbed wire to which my sock and shoe were attached. It was only on further inspection that I could see it was not a baby bird but flesh torn from the calf muscle of my leg. There was in truth no pain and very little blood, and having walked home I washed the wound and wrapped it in a handkerchief. I didn't tell my mum, and eventually the wound healed without any real problems, but it could have been much worse as you might have guessed. The crow's egg that I had so carefully brought down from the nest was smashed to smithereens.

At the height of my egg collection I had amassed some 240 eggs, a collection much increased by my passion for the eggs of rooks and carrion crows. One of the most difficult eggs to find was that of a cuckoo (a bird I have heard only once in the last 25 years). It was a very common visitor when I was a boy. Its song was bright, crisp and unmistakeable, but finding one of its eggs was something of a challenge. Every young egg collector wanted one. When I eventually found this elusive egg it was nestling among a clutch of hedge sparrow's eggs (more generally known today as the dunnock). As I separated the hedge and lent across to check the nest's contents, there among the delightful turquoise coloured eggs of the hedge sparrow I saw the cuckoo's egg, a densely mottled greenish brown and such a contrast in colour. I was overjoyed, and carefully extracted the egg from the nest with great care. Then with equal care I pierced the top and bottom of the egg, blew the yolk out, then wrapped the egg in cotton wool, placed it in one of Dad's old tobacco tins and made my way home.

As I walked home I was thinking that I had done the hedge sparrow a service, for had the egg hatched, the cuckoo chick would instinctively have removed all the sparrow's eggs from the nest.

On another day Alan and I set off through Compton Martin woods in search of more eggs and to visit in particular several rookeries located beyond the woods and into the Mendip Hills. Our route was unplanned.

After several hours of walking with little luck on the nesting front we came across John Davis (who in later life was a great friend of John Potter, my brother-in-law). Quite where we were I do not know and how I came to be astride a rather large grey mare is even more of mystery, as I had never ridden a horse before. In truth I was not astride the horse but sat bareback over its neck with just a set of reins.

At first the horse was well behaved and Alan and John walked calmly alongside, but then it started to trot, and then canter. "Whoa girl, whoa!" I heard John shout. I followed suit in my most manly of voices, but at 10 years of age it was not so effective. We were coming to a five-bar gate, and as the horse reached it it planted its front feet in the ground and stopped dead. I became airborne and landed some eight or ten feet the other side of the gate. The ground was soft and so was the landing - no pain and no breaks. But the horse was off and running and it took three hours to catch the damn thing. Then it took Alan and me another two hours to get home. We arrived just after seven in the evening, having left at nine in the morning. I got a real earful from my mother and was sent to bed immediately and told no play for a week, not a good end to the day.

At around 7.15 my friend Dave House knocked on the door asking for me, only to be told I was in bed. He handed mother a jackdaw's egg from a nest in the tower of Compton Martin Church, his dad being the local churchwarden. Mother brought the egg upstairs. I was cheered by this event. The egg was predominantly blue with black dashes and spots, with a hint of grey and khaki specks, larger than a mistle thrush's egg but smaller than a partridge egg. I placed it accordingly in the line of eggs, shifting the others up one place to accommodate it. There was room perhaps for four more eggs in this box.

I was tired and once in bed fell asleep very quickly. The house arrest was rescinded the following morning. Mum was such a softy.

When I was about thirteen I took a young jackdaw from the chimney of an old derelict house and kept it as a pet. I had to teach the young fellow to fly. I lifted it as high in the air as I could and it flapped its wings and flew a few yards. This process was repeated for several days until finally it could fly like the best of jackdaws. By instinct or what I don't know, but it would simply return to my shoulder whenever it was tired of flying. I don't remember what I called it but I am guessing it must have been Jack. Its name may escape me, but its passion for ripping wallpaper off bedroom walls does not. Any neighbour leaving their bedroom window open would soon discover what Jack was capable of. In the end I had to give the bird to a friend in the next village, but I don't think the habit stopped.

In those long summers of my schooldays, you had six or seven weeks to fill. The Boy Scouts use to camp next to Chapman's Farm in what is now the gardens of the Ring O' Bells pub. This provided us local lads with a touch of aggravated fun, as their arrival coincided with the early ripening of apples in Chapman's adjacent orchard. We use to bombard them with apples, five of us and possibly forty of them, but we had the lion's share of the apples. Direct hits really did hurt, black eyes often resulted and occasionally a right good scrap ensued, spoilt only by the Scoutmaster's intervention.

On other days we found more mischief with one of my sister's toys, a black woolly lamb. At a distance it looked remarkably like a cat, so I hatched a plan for the entertainment of the boys from the Buildings. We tied a long piece of string around the neck of the lamb, placed it on one side of the road, then walked across the road laying the string on the road behind us, hid behind the bus shelter and waited for a car to come down the road. Cars were less frequent in those days, so you had to be alert. The winner was the lad who could make a car skid the farthest. It was fabulous fun until the occasion when a driver ran over the pseudo cat, trapping it under his front wheel. The driver was out of the car in a flash, rope spotted, expletives soaring above the bus shelter, car door slammed. We were under the barbed wire quicker than a flash of lightning. He was as mad as a hatter, but we are away. And you know what, the blighter took our cat.

Falling out of trees, raising jackdaws, being ripped by blackthorns as you attempted to reach a jay's nest or getting soaked to the waist as you waded into a lake to collect a great crested grebe's egg was all part of the colourful scene of bird nesting. My next nesting adventure however was particularly intoxicating for me.

When I was thirteen a school friend called Pete George, who lived on a farm near Blagdon Lake, told me there was a swan's nest on the edge of the lake near his dad's farm in Ubley. It had been a lifetime's ambition to have a swan's egg, and now there seemed a real chance of bringing this to fruition.

I got to Pete's around 4.30 in the afternoon and we took little more than 15 minutes to reach the hedge bordering the lake. The nest was in a stumpy willow bush. It was impressively large, even from a distance, and partially hidden by the reeds. The swan that was sitting on the eggs looked magnificent.

Pete said he would keep a lookout while I went out to the nest. Crawling through the hedge and walking through the reeds bent double, I reached the nest in about five minutes. As I raised my body to full height the swan was looking directly at me, displaying no nerves or fear. She simply looked at me from five feet away, even more majestic now.

I approached the nest and with great care pushed the swan slightly off it with my trusted hazel stick. There were six light green eggs, magnificently large, and excitement filled every fibre of my body.

The swan stood up but was not moving from the nest. When I reached in and took one egg she hissed angrily. Then I broke my own rules and took a second. The swan was very agitated, but as I withdrew she sat quietly back down on the nest. My excitement hardly contained, I started walking back to the hedge.

I had not gone more than a few yards when over my shoulder I heard a noise like a siren. The cob (male) swan had seen me and was flying furiously towards me, the sound of its wings loud and urgent. Just as it was about to hit me, I dived full length into the reeds carefully holding the eggs one in each hand. In my excitement I had forgotten all about the female swan's partner (the pen) and I had left my trusted nesting stick back at the nest so had nothing to protect myself with.

I lay quietly in the wet reeds, heart pumping, excitement and fear surging through my veins. I knew I would have to keep very low and still for some time. The cob made two more passes before I could move and finally the hedge was in reach. The journey from hedge to nest had taken five minutes, the return journey almost an hour. My clothes were completely black and almost all of me was soaked and smelly. I had literally crawled along the reed bed on knees and elbows to avoid the swan and protect the eggs I had stolen.

It was the finest nesting day of my life - excitement, danger, triumph and all for free. Life really can give you some unforgettable treats. That summer I returned to the lake with Peter to witness those swans and the three beautiful cygnets they had raised.

With my mate Alan I shared a second hobby, stranger than nesting - racing snails. On a summer's day after a shower we would walk the hedgerows looking for new snails to add to our racing stock. Much of the time we raced each others' snails against one another, while sometimes I played with them for hours on my own. We raced them on old panes of glass moistened to aid the snail's passage, all in the wash house at my home. Even in my sixties as I walk the dogs on a damp summer's day, I look into the hedgerows and see the snails with their variety of colour and remember with fondness those boyhood days.

A third hobby was shared by Alan and me, along with Roly Tossell, Chris Tovey and sometimes Dave House and Ray Mitch. All of us lived in the Buildings except Chris, who lived in the centre of the village. Our hobby was racing hand-made model boats, hand-carved from scraps of wood, mostly four to six inches long and never more than two inches wide. They were sometimes pointed at both ends, sometimes pointed at the front and rounded at the rear, and occasionally a hull was carved. We would sandpaper the wood to a very fine finish and then in biro write our favorite names on the boats. It is a source of amazement that even now I recall some of those names. Alan's best boats were named Vanwall 2 and BRM, famous Formula One cars of the late fifties. Chris's best boat was Huckleberry Hound from the cartoon (this boat won almost every race), while my favourite was Never Say Die, which I actually had painted blue. It was named after a race horse.

The races took place outside Chapman's Farm, where there was a small gully running at the edge of the road (my sister Kate tells me that in November 2012 the whole area was flooded because the ditch was filled in by the council, who had to come along and dig it out again. It had been running fine for 100 years). It took run-off water from the hill above and was about a foot and half wide and ran for about 75 yards, in part through a large drainpipe which was cemented over to allow tractors and cattle into the adjacent field. When the boats exited the drainpipe there was 10 metres to go to the winning line. The finishing post was simply a stick placed across the gully. You had to grab the boats quickly after this point before they disappeared under the main road and followed a gully which was known as the 'drang' and eventually flowed into Chew Valley Lake.

We would enter two boats each into a race if there were only four of us, but when all six were playing it was one each. We simply dropped them into the water from one hand (it mattered not whose hand), with the winning boat going through to the final, and eight races before the final was reached. The routine was always the same, just the number of lads participating and the handmade boats varying from day to day. The game was very economical in terms of cost, great fun and had the added advantage of much exercise, and of course when you had made the winning boat, much pride. Unfortunately I can only ever remember my boats coming second.

Alan Gould, with whom I enjoyed such great boyhood moments, was unfortunately killed at the age of 21 in a tragic crane accident, when the crane jib swung out of control, catching Alan across the back of his head. That was just two months after he had become a father. He was a great friend and we enjoyed many good times together. As young children and in our early teens some of the lads, including Alan's younger brother, had mocked us for the snail hobby, but I never felt any embarrassment about it and we both enjoyed the simple competition of racing those snails.

It wasn't all snails and bird nesting. There was boating as well, and football was already a passion. We played in the field behind our house, mostly five-a-side, of all ages from eight to 15, nearly every Sunday. In the summer it was cricket. Such was my enthusiasm for football that I nagged my father week after week to let me go with him to watch the 1956 FA Cup final between Man City and Birmingham City, not to Wembley. This final was to be watched at Walter Field's house. The Fields had the only house in the Buildings with a TV, and I sat there with 16 men, on a small stool, enthralled with the game. It was made famous by the fact that Bert Trautmann, ex-German prisoner of war and Manchester City goalkeeper, broke his neck and played on for the final 16 minutes, Man City winning 3-1.

In 1957 mum rented a small television with a twelve inch screen. Today my sister Kate lives in and owns the house that was Walter Field's.

At school it all changed on reaching eleven years of age. I first attended St. Bernadette's, a Roman Catholic school at Whitchurch on the edge of Bristol. It was a brand new school, but unfortunately because of the travel I had to miss the last lesson every day, and the education authorities said this was unacceptable. I spent nearly seven months at home while my mother disputed the decision. She had been converted to the Catholic faith on marrying Dad and her faith was very strong. Eventually however I attended Chew Valley Secondary Modern, where there were some 430 pupils. The catchment area was Dundry, Winford, Felton, Lulsgate, Pensford, Stanton Drew, Chew Magna, Chew Stoke, Bishop Sutton, East and West Harptree, Compton Martin and Ubley, with some small catchment areas in between like Coley and Nempnett Thrubwell.

Chew Valley, like St Bernadette's, was a very new school, having been built only the previous year. Here there was no football, only rugby, not a game I particularly liked playing. In my year there were four groups graded from A to D (in later years this was known as streaming), while all other years had three grades. I understand our year was part of the post-war baby boom (a bit of restocking I guess). Initially I was put in the C grade, but after some form of assessment exam I was put in the B group. As an aside, while in the C group I sat next to Mike Potter (not knowing of course some thirteen years later that he would become my brother-in-law).

Now for a moment back to the sport and rugby. We played rugby once a week and it lasted the whole afternoon session, with some training such as kicking, passing, scrummaging techniques and then a game. We often split into two groups. I recall how much I disliked the game and in the early weeks I would not pick the ball up. I didn't mind tackling and the scrummaging was OK, but when you picked the ball up every bugger jumped on you. So I decided it was best to kick the ball - not the done thing, you know. I was cured of this kicking problem on the third afternoon of playing when the sports master bellowed across the pitch 'pick the ball up Boyd or you're going for the slipper!' When the ball next ran free, I instinctively kicked it like a football. The whistle went and I was instructed to walk to the changing rooms to collect a size 10 plimsoll and deliver it to the sports master, who told me to bend over, whereupon he brought the plimsoll sharply down across my buttocks, saying 'I'll keep it for a while just in case you should forget', but of course I never did.

At 15 years of age and in my last few months at school I played my one and only game for the school rugby team at fullback, which I actually rather enjoyed. I was quite proud to wear the school colours of green and white hoops. Throughout my school days I was a regular member of the rugby and cricket house teams, our house being Rodney, while the others were Hauteville, Bilby and Moreton. Moreton was the village which was evacuated and flooded when Chew Valley lake was filled. My first love however remained football, and I arranged many local matches against Ubley and West Harptree. There were no referees and scores like 14-8 were not uncommon. Fouls were never given and often the numbers on each side were uneven, but I looked forward to them with immense anticipation and excitement and we won as many as we lost.

In the last two years of school the sports master, Doug Wooding, would referee Rovers v City (Bristol) football matches. I played in the Rovers team, hence my life long support of Bristol Rovers. The lads were two to one in favour of City, which made it easier to get into the Rovers side, though in truth we often won perhaps because our side rarely changed and we became a real team.

In my final year at school I suffered a real sporting disappointment, in the school cross country championship. Having finished 56th and 9th previously, I was determined to go out on a high before leaving school a few days later. I trained for a number of weeks with Eddie Whitfield, who lived at Chew Stoke. The cross country race set off towards Pagan's Hill, cut back along the riverside and around the edge of Chew Valley Lake, returning through Chew Stoke back to the school. Going into the last mile (I believe the total course was about five and half miles) Frank Barber, Eddy Whitfield and Derek Johnson were ahead of me. Unfortunately for him, Frank went the wrong way. I caught Eddie with half a mile to go and I was closing on Derek as we entered the main drive of the school, but the faster I ran so did he, and I had to settle for second place, a great disappointment. Derek collapsed as he went over the line and I ended up carrying him to the changing rooms. He was tough but a skinny little bugger, so he weighed very little.

The next day, the penultimate day of my school life, I recall having to report to Mr Wright, our maths teacher, for punishment for some form of misdemeanour. When I failed to do so he came looking for me at lunchtime, and I simply hid under the dinner table. Mr Wright noted the empty space and told the lads having dinner, "Tell Boyd that due to his excellent run yesterday and his sporting act at the end of the race, his slate is wiped clean and he can come out from under the table once I have left, and not before".

In the years at school I had entered the dreaded Deputy Headmaster's cupboard for corrective punishment on quite a few occasions, including once for sticking a pin in a boy's bottom as we queued to catch the school bus home and once for fighting a boy called Malcolm Hassen in class, when we were sent to stand outside the classroom door. The Deputy Headmaster patrolled the corridors of the school during lesson time, and should you be found outside the classroom it would be deemed you had committed a misdemeanour worthy of four obligatory whacks with his favorite slipper in the cupboard of correction.

Mr Guard, the Deputy Head, wore small steel caps on the tips of his shoes and his gait was always recognisable. As we stood outside the door, the sound was unmistakeable. If he turned left at the end of the corridor and walked up the stairs we would be following him back down to the cupboard. Opposite where we stood was the teachers' staff room, so I suggested to Malc that we should hide in there for a few minutes. If we were caught the punishment would increase from the obligatory four to six. Four really hurt but six was downright painful,. We took the risk and got lucky.

On another occasion when I tore up someone's art paper, I was sent straight to the Headmaster for the cane, the offence deemed more serious than fighting. I can tell you it always hurt far more than I let on and I never let my parents know for fear of a second dose. The punishments however did me no harm. They served simply to reinforce the difference between right and wrong.

On my visit to the school some 45-plus years after leaving, I walked the classrooms of the original school. In the classroom with the roll call of those who had attended over the past 50 years I lingered momentarily and ruefully smiled as I realised this had been Mr Guard's classroom, and there was the cupboard door where you entered, bent over and took your punishment.

At the end of each school year all classes took an exam in Religious Knowledge, History, Geography, Music, English, Rural Science, General Science, Maths and Technical Drawing. There were no exams for Art or Woodworking. In the third year exams (when I was 14) I had a moment of good fortune and brightness and finished top of the class in 7 out of the 9 subjects, only Music and Technical Drawing letting me down. I could not tell the difference between a semiquaver and an ice cream cone when it came to music, and in the technical drawing exam I finished fifth. We had been taught the subject for one year only and had been learning alongside the A Stream, who had had a two-year start, so I considered this a good result.

My school report for this year, sadly now lost, carried my dislike of the expectations of those in authority, be they teachers, directors of business or whoever assumed authority over me. The history teacher wrote: "Michael would do even better were he not to challenge every written word and much of what is said". I recall her anger every time I asked or questioned historic issues and even suggested that her views or those of the historians might not be correct. Such temerity from one so young! The history teacher really did not like me.

I was always a bit of a rebel and never wore a school uniform. I always wore jeans, and some outlandish ones at that, and occasionally my shirts were a bit oddly patterned. When it was prize-giving day, Mr Guard said that photos would be taken (they might be used in the local newspaper) and it would be rather nice if I turned up in a white shirt and black or grey trousers to receive my award. The books I had chosen were on birds. My interest in birds had extended beyond the basics of egg collection, and I was fascinated by the various nest constructions and materials and would nearly always know which bird had made the nest before seeing the eggs or the bird. I was also very aware of various habitats birds used for nesting and feeding and could recognise them by their song or the noise they made in flight.

Mr Guard's statement was only a request. Had it been an instruction, I would simply have said no, but it was reasonable and I answered in the affirmative. There was pleasure on his face and a genuine "thank you" on the day of the presentation. Mr Guard was very proud of his school. I met him many years later at the 50th Anniversary celebration. He was still very upright and approaching ninety years of age, and it was good to see him. I held no grudges over the whackings I had received in his punishment cupboard, only genuine respect for a very good teacher, a good deputy head and an upright person.

Away from school, at about 12 years of age I began to visit Chapman's Farm in the middle of the village with my next door neighbour, Roly Tossell. It was very interesting and I became fascinated by the process of milking cattle. It was not long before I was helping Roger (the owner's son) to do the milking. Some cattle had to be spanned (rear legs tied) during milking as they kicked rather violently. Spanning a cow for the first time was a bit scary. The cow might lash out suddenly, and that really hurt if you got caught. She might also become very nervous and do a large dump, and as you were somewhat adjacent to the rear end this could be the absolute pits. You had to move with extreme speed under such circumstances to avoid a dousing in fresh cow manure.

One of the cows which required spanning was called Cryer, a beautiful black and white spotted cow, and I decided to try to soften her behaviour so she could be milked without the restraint. At each milking she was given a small handful of cow cake, which she ate quite willingly from my hand. Then I took to grooming her, and eventually after washing her udder prior to attaching the milking machine (without restraint) I went the whole hog and attached the vacuum machine, which milked her without the span. She never moved a muscle, and I never put the rope on her again.

My interest in the individual milk production of each cow led me to weigh the milk of each cow for a year and record their output. Roger found this information very useful when he came to retaining calves for the purpose of herd replacement. At this time I also started smoking, aided and abetted by my mate Alan Gould and later reinforced as payment for milking the cattle. Roger Chapman was an avid kart racer, racing mainly at Shipham. I would milk the cattle one Sunday and another lad the next, and the weeks when we weren't milking we would go to the kart racing. For the milking we received 10 cigarettes. Having started smoking at 11 I finally stopped at 58. More of my last cigarette later in the story.

Of course by the time I was thirteen I was regularly driving the tractor in the fields, chain harrowing (basically raking the grass) and of course rolling it ahead of summer growth. This helped a great deal later on when it came to driving a car. I had the chance to drive an old Austin Seven around Chris Tovey's orchard. his mum and dad had bought him the car for a birthday present and about four of us raced it around the orchard to see who was the fastest.

As we entered our teenage years most of the lads, myself included, remained very young at heart. We built massive dens in Compton Martin woods, some with boundaries of hazel which grew into hedges. The den would be made of woven sticks infilled with branches, the roof covered in moss collected from the wood. Such dens would take months to build and might last several years. On other occasions we made camp fires and cooked sausages provided by Roger from the farm. We all had bows made from hazel and many of us made spears, carefully carved and sometimes polished. Many a javelin-throwing contest ensued and much pride was gained for throwing the farthest. These were the pursuits of country lads, always simple and nearly always enjoyable.

The farm was a focal point for much of our youthful pleasure. The fields above the farm house provided super tobogganing slopes during snow-laden winters, the stream that ran alongside the road behind the farm great boat racing facilities. The road which led to the quarry was a racetrack for our bicycles.

This road was little used and afforded us one very hairy moment. My DIY skills had now developed beyond making forts for my tin soldiers to building trolleys and trailers, possible because at the farm there was a workbench and many simple tools. Over the course of a month I built a trolley using wood from an old chest and various pieces of wood from around the farm. Wheels had come from a pram and the nuts, bolts and screws courtesy of Roger. The steering was a bit Heath Robinson; holes were punched through the front plate, to which the wheels were attached and rope threaded through on either side. Pulling left or right gave you good control over direction. The trolley provided room for two kids, so I set about creating a trailer to carry a further four.

One quiet Sunday afternoon in August the six of us set sail for the top of the road known locally as the Combe. Our intention was to ride the trolley from top to bottom, the road having a one in 10 incline. As the builder I got to steer, of course.

We sat like dominoes aboard our trolley. At first our speed was gentle and I maintained a position about five feet from the left-hand bank. The trolley gathered momentum very quickly, and in a flash we were past the first few houses on the left we felt a tremendous rush of air and a great degree of excitement. Then the whole trolley began to rock and the steering ropes burned my hands. We climbed the bank on the left with no loss of speed, but now we were sitting at an odd angle. After another thirty feet the rope was wrenched from my left hand, a wheel snapped and the trolley turned virtually upside down. Now we all knew we were going to crash. My head hit the road, then my elbow and finally my right knee. Much the same happened to those riding behind me. The trolley was destroyed, flesh bloodied and bruised, clothes torn. The ride lasted less than three minutes, but I will always remember it.

Roger's brother Rex was a real sportsman and we played cricket in the farmyard with him for hours (that same yard today is full of houses). I went to watch Somerset play cricket with Rex, who was in the RAF and based for some time at Lyneham. On one occasion he was called back to make some repairs to a Hercules, and I went with him. It was a great day out at 14 (a trip to Widnes and two to Weston Super Mare were the extent of my travel at that time).

Roly Tossell and I had a full tour of the camp, and we were allowed to go into the hanger where Rex was working on the Hercules and climb the platform to the top, which of course was the tip of the tail wing. It seemed miles from the ground. To top it off we were given a full lunch and a couple of chocolate bars by the mess chef. It was a great day.

Saturday afternoons were also good fun on the farm as we gathered around the TV set with Roger and his dad Herbie to watch the wrestling before we went out to do the milking. Looking back I guess the wrestling was a bit farcical, but we all really enjoyed it.

By now I was 15 and my boyhood and schooldays

were both coming to a close. When I left school in April 1962, the first thing to do was to find a job.

# CHAPTER TWO

# Cows and courtship

I was helped in the task of finding my first job by my ex Deputy Head. Mum, God bless her, had got me an interview at the local sack factory. The owners were Catholics and had often given us a lift to church at East Harptree on Sunday mornings. The interview went OK, but the job appeared to involve a great deal of manual labour and very little else and had absolutely no appeal. The pay would be three pounds 13 shillings per week. My schooling reports gave little promise of an Einstein, but I did consider myself too good to hump sacks.

Fortunately for me Mr Guard had arranged an interview for me at the Cow & Gate Dairy at Chew Stoke (now redeveloped with houses and a large GP surgery). It was on the bus route and possible to cycle there, about five and half miles. Mr Guard explained that I would be the first boy to get a job as a lab technician at this dairy, and if I were successful at interview I must not let the school down. He had also explained (thank heavens) to the Dairies Deputy Manager, Mr Nash, who interviewed me in the absence of the chemist, that I had a rather offbeat approach to clothing. I turned up for the interview in my smartest clothes, a brand new pair of red and black striped jeans and a purple open-neck shirt covered in pictures of nude ladies. Well, I thought I looked OK - and I got the job.

The pay seemed good at four pounds three shillings a week. To give you some measure of value, back then you could buy eight pints of beer for £1 or 10 gallons of petrol for £2. I left school on the Friday and started work on the Monday, two weeks before Easter. With my first pay packet, I bought my sisters, Kate, who was 12, and Jenny, 11, the largest Easter eggs you could buy. They were delighted, and both I believe recall the event to this day.

I was to spend nearly eleven years at this location, eventually moving into training, and on one occasion I did a spot on Radio Bristol about the modernisation of the dairy, my three minutes of fame. I spoke without an accent of any kind - never before and never since. I was interviewed by Sara Pitt, who I knew socially as a girlfriend of one of my mates, and we partied at her flat on a few occasions. The other technicians were mostly girls. In fact one, Jenny, was to become my first love and we lost our virginity together. She went into hairdressing six months after I joined the lab team and the romance lasted almost two and half years. She lived at Morledge, at the very top end of Chew Magna on the road to the Pony and Trap, where we often went for a beer.

On the subject of virginity, my mind is momentarily drawn to a day not long after I started working when mother had asked to me to collect a chicken from Weaver's farm on the way home. Stopping at the farm, I unfolded the leather bag given to me by mother to collect the chicken. It was almost dark as I left the bike at the top of the yard and walked towards the house. I immediately became aware of a collie dog, and was pretty sure its intentions towards me were not good. After eyeing me up for a short while it ran straight at me with teeth on full display. I raised the bag and belted the dog around the head as hard as I possibly could. It ran off and I continued towards the door, not giving the dog another thought.

Ten feet from the door I felt an excruciating pain in my backside. The dog had doubled back, crept up behind me and sunk its teeth good and proper into my rear end. It was bloody painful. I continued to the door and knocked.

Betty Weaver opened the door and I told her, "I've come to collect a chicken".

"You look a little flushed" she said. "Yes, your damn dog has just taken a chunk out of my backside." I replied.

"Well you had better come in take your trousers and pants down and I'll have a good look at you" she said.

If I was flushed before, I was now scarlet. "No no!" I protested. "I'll just give it a good rub."

Now I may have imagined her intentions, but the look of disappointment on her face suggested not. Betty must have been 33 or so and I was not quite ready to lose my virginity in such an unceremonious way.

I cycled home with a rather sore bum, mentioning not a word about the events to Mum. "You look a little flushed" she said. "Yes, too much exercise" I replied.

Now back to the girls at the lab, all about my age. Jenny emigrated to Australia. I fancied Judy quite a lot, but never got round to asking her out. She now lives in Canada, and Dot in New Zealand. The assistant chemist emigrated to Australia. Was it something I said? Only Christine Walker, who lives at Chewton Mendip, and I are still British residents of the staff of 62.

In the winter of 1962/63 we had nearly three months of snow. Jenny had come to our house for Boxing Day; her stepdad had dropped her off on his motor bike. The snow fell so heavily that neither her stepdad nor the bus service could use the roads, so Jenny stayed the night, sleeping in my bed. Sadly I was downstairs on the sofa. For three months I rode my bike to work on roads that were covered in a hard crust of frozen snow. I fell off many times, but rarely hurt myself. I would catch the bus to Chew Magna to see Jenny, but invariably have to walk or hitchhike home as the last bus never made it to Chew Magna. I enjoyed tremendous tobogganing every weekend with the lads from the Buildings, and we played football on the frozen surface of the pond which can still be found in the middle of the village as you drive through Compton Martin.

Returning to my new job, some three months into my life as a lab tech, Roger, the farmer I went kart racing with, had a bad back injury, so I used to milk the 25 cows, starting at six in morning, and then cycle the five and half miles to work. The third week into this routine the Laboratory Supervisor (not popular with me, or most of us) called me aside and pointed out that my clothes were often covered in cow manure and the smell was not pleasant. I had never given it a thought, but from then on I did change on arrival at work.

My interest in football was still very keen and eventually I decided that I would try and start a football club. At sixteen you are full of confidence. Harptree United had a very good team and Blagdon just a couple of miles to the west was also a pretty reasonable team. Eventually, after setting up a village pontoon club to fund the costs of running the team, we had enough money to support a football club. I walked the village every Sunday morning collecting sixpence from every participating member, over 150 people in all, with some purchasing two tickets, Roly Tossell did the chore every fifth Sunday when I had to work. The winners, namely those whose selected football team was first to get 21 goals, received 40% of the pot, while the rest was retained to fund the club.

Today it seems unlikely that £300 a year could

sustain a football team, but alongside players' contributions it was more than enough. At that time a new amateur football league, Bristol Regional League, was starting up and I applied for us to join. It was quite a task at 16 to get the club up and running, but I persuaded Mr Kelson, a sales rep and member of our pontoon club, to become Treasurer and Jack Tossell, Roly's uncle, to become Chairman. I would act as the Club Secretary. A ground was found, and the village hall with a tin bath was our changing room. I managed to get my old sports master, Doug Wooding, to allow the club to purchase, via his school discount arrangements, all our shirts, football nets, balls and a line-marking machine. A lad who worked at the local sawmills in Ubley got us the goalposts totally free of charge.

Sadly the club lasted less than three years, but we got to be second in the league that first season, finally finishing tenth. The club was also solvent and somewhere in the Nat West Bank is £39 belonging to Compton Martin AFC. But like today's lesser clubs we could not keep our best players and finally we could not keep our worst.

I then joined Harptree United. I was to play only a handful of games for the first team. Though I absolutely adored football, in truth I was a very average player. There was however to be one big season and one big game. Our reserve team was pretty decent and we entered the Temple Colston Cup (a league cup competition still running in 2011). We played in

Division 4 of the Church of England League, our first team played in Division 1 and were champions on many occasions. They also entered the Temple Colston Cup. In the first round we drew Henbury OBs Reserves, who were top of our league and unbeaten all season; they were all super-fit kids. We played them off the park, but could not put the ball in the net. Eventually we beat them one nil.

In the second round we played, Temple Cloud Reserves of Division 3, a bit of a local derby, we won by 4 goals to 1, and I missed a penalty getting closer to the corner post than the goal mouth. Our keeper was from Temple Cloud and I remember him going ballistic when I missed. Round 4 brought a Division 2 side, as did round 5. In this game we played the first half with 10 men, the eleventh man turning up just before the second half kicked off as his car had broken down. We played well. Harvey's Wines were top of Division 2 at the time and we scored the only goal 10 minutes into the game, running out, I thought, worthy winners.

Now we were at the semi-final stage. The final in our day was played at Bristol City's ground at Ashton Gate and our first team were still in the cup. The other semi-finalists were Blagdon and Norton Hill Rangers and we draw Blagdon at home.

This game was played in December. The weather had been very cold and ours was one of the few matches being played that day, so a remarkable crowd (around 300 people) had turned out to watch. Blagdon of course was less than four miles away and the first team were not playing, so our entire first team, along with those from many other local sides, came to watch, plus a very big contingent from Blagdon. We had not lost one of our previous 19 games and were second in our own division, so we were very confident and the thought of playing at Ashton Gate, against our first team was a big fillip. Moreover our centre forward had been a regular first team player the previous season before injury caused a long layoff and he was exceptionally good (his son played briefly for Bristol City). Blagdon also had a very good centre forward called Beverley Ash who stood 6' 3" and fifteen stone and was fit and very mobile. He was good with both his feet and his head. Their right winger was a cousin of Chris Garland of Bristol City and Chelsea fame, and their inside right, Westlake, worked with my sister at the local shop in Blagdon.

The game kicked off to a huge cheer from the crowd. Casting aside modesty of any kind, I was to have my best-ever day on a football pitch. Every sinew in my in body was like a tightly-wound elastic band and I was truly pumped up.

I was playing at left half, a midfield role I guess in today's modern game, and for a year or two I had been doing a great deal of weightlifting (strength lifting to be exact) and it made a real difference on the football pitch. The game was less than 10 minutes old when Bev Ash, the Blagdon centre forward, received a through ball from their right half, Tony Badger. Bev gathered it well and was around our centre half in a couple of strides and about to shoot when I hit him bloody hard from the side (shoulder charge I guess). He went flying, the ball was at my feet and I cleared to David Cook, our right winger, who took the ball down the line, crossed, and Andy Marshall, our centre forward, met it with his head - one nil to Harptree United Reserves.

Just before half time Blagdon equalized, and 15 minutes into the second half Bev Ash was almost through again when I dropped my shoulder into his chest with some force. He looked a little surprised as I offered my hand to give him a lift up. Bev said "I am too quick for you Mike", and smiled at me (well, I thought, you are the one on your ass) but from the free kick Blagdon took the lead.

We were not finished. I recall putting in some heavyweight tackles on their inside right (my sister's colleague at the shop) and clashing badly with Tony Badger, their right half, who threatened to bust my jaw. While he was whingeing, I slipped the ball to Brian Speed, who rounded their left half and scored a pretty good goal so it was 2-2. Blagdon on the attack. I stopped Garland in his tracks and he tumbled to the floor, the ball ran into touch off Garland, I took the throw and Andy Marshall picked up the ball and fired a quick pass to Cookie on the wing, who in turn waltzed past two of their defenders and delivered a perfect cross to Andy Marshall, who scored a really fabulous goal - Harptree United Reserves 3, Blagdon 2. The crowd was ecstatic and the noise unbelievable. The feeling of joy was almost indescribable.

But within seconds I suffered the first of two major cramp attacks. I had run and run, but Blagdon in the end were simply too strong for us, running out 5-3 winners. The headline in the *Green 'Un*, the local Bristol sports paper of the day, read 'Blagdon put a stop to an all-Harptree United Temple Colston Cup Final'.

My sister's workmate said I was the dirtiest player he had ever played against, but in truth, I just had a good game, almost certainly my best. I certainly played in front of the biggest crowd I had ever experienced.

My footballing days did not last as long as I would have liked, as work and many other things got in the way. I played a few games for Clutton and Stanton Drew about four years after I gave up playing for Harptree United, but it did not work out and in any event none would ever compare to that December game. Later I was to take up Badminton and table skittles, the latter not really being a sport and confined to about 16 pubs in and around Wrington. This game did provide the Bell Ubley pub team with immense fun and great rivalry in the local area. We were a good team, almost all in our early twenties, and we became league champions, knockout cup holders and individual and doubles champions. I note from the *Chew Valley Gazette* of 2010 that the game is still being played in the area and several individual winners of that year were once members of the Bell-Ubley team.

Bell-Ubley reached a number of table skittles Knock Cup Finals and in the first the captain paired me with Christine. In contrast to our badminton games, we played pretty well together, both being decent players. The game was rather simple, eight people playing in pairs, each pair playing three legs against the opponents. The first to score 91 exactly won the leg. Christine and I had rather a good night. You got three throws on your turn, nine skittles, maximum 27. I scored the maximum on five occasions, Christine scored 26 twice. Neither of us apart from the last throw (the getting out throw/exact number needed) scored under 18. We won our legs 3-0 and contributed to an 8-4 win on the night.

Returning to my teenage years, at 18 I bought my first car, a Morris Ten, year of production 1948. It was black and the top speed was 58mph. It cost £16, and when I went to insure it the cost was £16 11 shillings and 9 old pence (£16.58). I simply did not have the one and nine, so Jimmy Raps, the insurance rep, let me have the insurance for £16 10 shillings.

After many years of driving the tractor and racing an old Austin Seven around Chris Tovey's orchard, driving came as second nature. I put the L plates on for a month, then dismissed them and drove for the next two years or so without them. I could not afford to take my test, and guess what, when I did I failed (I pulled up for a pigeon, doing an unrequested emergency stop and throwing the examiner's papers everywhere). I passed second time, just before I was 21.

The old car was great, and when the battery was flat it had a starting handle which could be used to turn the engine over and start the car. I tell you this because during my footballing days I snapped a tendon in my ankle (ironically playing against Courage Brewing, who I was to work for later in life) and ended up not being able to walk for some while. I did however still drive the car, despite not having a full licence yet. On one occasion with the battery flat I turned the car engine over on one leg and with the assistance of a stone lodged on the throttle pedal to make sure the engine, once started, kept going, and off I went to see someone at East Harptree. As I drove through West Harptree I attempted to brake, but the pedal would not move and I nearly had a bad accident. The stone I had used to keep the car ticking over had rolled under the brake pedal and lodged there. It was a scary moment.

The job as a lab technician was fine, and seemed not to interfere with my sport and social life. It just paid the bills, though every week I was in hock for my cigarettes. I used to get them from the Dairy Office. Each packet after Wednesday went on the slate and I paid for them on the Friday.

I had started college a year after starting my job in the laboratory, studying for my City & Guilds. Having achieved the pass mark in year one, I gave up half way through year two - too many other things going on. Despite this I was given at 19 the position of Head Lab Technician, which meant I was in charge of all laboratory personnel in the absence of the chemist and had the task of dealing with irate farmers whose milk might have been rejected for consumption because of its keeping quality (gone sour before arrival) or it contained foreign substances, i.e. blood. The milk in those early days arrived in churns and a person known as a "sniffer" would lift the lid of every churn arriving at the dairy and literally sniff the contents and visually check the milk. Should the sniffer detect anything out of the ordinary, the churn would be pulled from the conveyor belt and the lab would test the milk for any abnormalities. A good sniffer could tell if the milking parlour had been painted, tarmac laid or the cows had been grazing too close to wild garlic.

Just over a year later I moved out of the laboratory to become Site Trainer in the dairy. At the time the Industrial Training Boards were becoming quite important and companies received reasonable sums of money from the Government if they could demonstrate that they had good, complete training plans.

I learned every operation in the dairy, including the sniffer role (I was made for this role on account of my large nose and very strong sense of smell) and on completion of the training I became responsible for training all new employees and those transferring across different operating disciplines. In the sixties turnover was quite high with almost full levels of employment. At one point, during Labour's time in power in the sixties, unemployment nationally was just 164,000, a remarkable figure.

The job was reasonably well paid. I cannot recall the exact amount, but it paid enough for me to buy my first decent car (a Ford Anglia, and guess what, it had previously been owned by Courage Limited, a rep's car I believe). The job was to be instrumental in eventually launching my management career, but there would be a few bumps along the way before that career even got started.

Where my leisure life and holidays with my mates fitted in is more difficult to recall than I imagined, but when I was around 20 we borrowed a large army tent from my mate's brother-in-law and headed off to Cornwall, six of us in total. My recollection of this holiday is sparked by the events that took place on the cliff top where we pitched the tent. The days were gloriously warm, but the nights on top of that cliff were really cold and we kept a small burner going for as long as the fuel lasted. It was only methylated spirits and gave off little heat, but it broke the chill. As we sat late into the night, some almost asleep, others swapping boys' stories and enjoying a few bottles of beer, the burner started to flicker. I picked up the meths and topped up the burner, turning the bottle upright. I felt the coldness of the meths run down my arm, followed instantly by flames. For some inexplicable reason, I attempted to put it out by violently swinging the bottle through the air in an arc while maintaining my grip on it. The methylated spirits gushed out ahead of the flames, hitting one corner of the tent, and like a rainbow arched its way to the other corner.

Some of the lads had been nodding off, but they soon woke up with the tent on fire. Panic ensued as we all dashed for the exit. Incredibly, I had no burns from the meths flames and the tent and contents suffered zero damage, but the burner was not lit again.

My twenty-first birthday came surprisingly quickly, and life with the fair sex was bubbling along quite nicely. Weekends were mostly spent in the Bristol dance halls, the Glen on the Downs (now a private hospital), the Locarno (round the back of the Hippodrome) and the Mandrake Club in the city centre underneath Park Street. In truth the latter club was for the up and coming snobs of my era. I recall on one occasion at the Locarno I had been sitting down chatting up this girl and asked her if she would like to dance. "Yes please" came the answer, but as we stood up it was apparent that she was quite a bit taller than me. Immediately she said "I am not dancing with you". I suggested she should take off her shoes, but it was a no go and I went off to the bar for a drink with my ego bruised. It was the first time in my life I had realized how short I was. But soon I was to meet the second love of my life, the girl who became my first wife.

Back in 1968, the year of my 21st, the laws on drink driving had not arrived. I recall it must have been a Wednesday, as we were playing skittles at the Mill Inn at Butcombe. It was a drunken night, starting at the Bell, where the Landlord, Danny McNicol, gave me a shot of vodka and the lads bought me a couple of black and tans (cider and Guinness) before we set off for the Mill. They were close rivals of ours and we knew every member of their team. Drinks flowed all night, once they discovered that it was my birthday. I was outrageously drunk on leaving the pub. Steve Flower (who now owns the farm opposite where my grandmother's place once was - the one with the wonderful pond - now full of houses - evidently saved me from falling into the river just outside the door.

My mother hated drinking and some inner sense told me as I reached the back door that much of the liquid I had consumed that evening was about to reappear. I must have deposited the night's indulgence over the neighbour's wire fence, thus avoiding upsetting my mother, but as I did so I went with the flow over the fence myself. For a long while it was very difficult to stand up, but eventually, I somehow managed to return to our house, which after all was only next door, and find the back door key, which was hung in the outside toilet. Even more surprisingly I managed to unlock the door and let myself in.

When I woke the next morning my head was in total disarray. I made a coffee and felt immediately drunk. Slowly I washed and shaved and now suddenly I wondered where the car was - I could not possibly have driven home, could I? There were no keys anywhere.

When I looked outside, however, there was the car neatly parked against the kerb. By sheer chance I then spotted my car keys on the lawn next door, along with the mess I had left the previous evening. I collected and washed the keys and used an old watering can to clean up the neighbour's lawn. Then I drove to work. Two hours later I was home again, having been sick at least four times.

In 1968 I helped move my grandfather (Granfer Dick) from Magpie Alley, where I had spent so many happy hours, to a council bungalow, where he was to live out his life well into his eighties, despite having smoked 60 Woodbines a day. I had a Ford Anglia, and although my grandfather was not taking much with him it took an awful long time. Then the rain started to come down, and then it came down some more. On completion of the move I called into the Ring O' Bells at Compton Martin for a pint, but water was coming off the hills, entering through the back door of pub and running out of the front door.

When I got home our neighbours who lived in the dip below us were also suffering with floods. Her husband was helping at the pub, and try as I might, I could not divert the water. That evening, July 10 1968, the bridge at Pensford, just below where my son James and his wife Helen now live, was swept away in a torrent of water.

I took not a single day off. The dairy operated seven days a week and I worked six of them including every weekend. Over Christmas the cows did not stop producing so we had to work. On Tuesdays, my day off, I worked at Winford Market, ushering cattle into the selling ring after coding each animal by breed and gender. During my two weeks' annual holiday (we got a little less time off in the sixties and early seventies), I worked for Dury's, the milk hauliers, driving a lorry collecting milk in churns from the local farms. I can still roll two churns simultaneously almost forty years after leaving the industry. I find the churns at bygone stalls and instantly have a roll with them.

I had worked two years solid in order to buy a sports car, and was now able to buy a two-year-old blue Triumph Spitfire for £550. It had both a soft and a hard top.

I continued working for another four weeks at the market, but the job did not last before disaster struck. As I was driving home past the market, which at the time was based in the centre of Winford, almost next to the Waterloo pub, the last cow I had put into the selling ring jumped out and ran amok in the market and then onto the main road, where it leapt on top of my new car, causing serious damage to the bonnet, which had to be replaced. I did not work again at the market, though the owners did pay up via their insurance company.

The market was owned by King Miles, true blue Tories through and through, and I was a staunch Labour supporter. Every Tuesday while we were sorting the cattle a great political debate took place, really spicy and good fun. I could wind up the younger King Miles lads, Geoff King in particular, and one or two of the lasses who worked there, without effort. The arena of debate around politics can be so emotive and so delightfully aggravating.

New operations were now being introduced at the dairy, and I began working every other weekend ( no chore, after all I had previously worked every weekend) to accommodate the intake and despatch of milk tankers. My bachelor life was also about to change.

I met Christine in the Bell at Ubley, the axis of most of my social activity and that of all my mates. She had come in with Kenny Mitchell, a member of the table skittles team, and a few other friends of mine. On her second visit to the pub I chatted to her during the evening and towards the end of the evening I asked her on a date. She said yes. I simply cannot recall where we went, but on her next visit to the pub she had a bad crash on her way home between Compton Martin and West Harptree, just below the crossroads at Fairash, writing off her very first car, a smart Triumph Herald which had recently been sprayed in British Racing Green. We had not exchanged phone numbers, one good reason being that we did not have a phone at home and mobiles were of course yet to be invented. So it would be several weeks before I was to see Christine again. I did not even know where she lived, and in any case turning up at her home would not be the done thing after one date.

Barbara Tovey worked in the offices at the dairy and her son had been seeing Christine's identical twin sister Lol for some time, so Barbara was able to let me know how Christine was getting on.

It was three weeks before we met again, but the

romance was on and within 18 months I asked Christine to marry me. I proposed in the Spitfire while parked on the drive at Broomhill House, her home in Clutton. There was no immediate yes, and it was several days before I managed to persuade her. Our wedding was very traditional and took place at the Mendip Hotel, Blagdon. The owner, Fitty, was a personal friend of Christine's dad and his wife Maggie. The hotel at this time was very upmarket and was used by Edward Heath, the Tory Prime Minister, when staying in the area on a visit. The wedding was at St. Michael's Roman Catholic Church, East Harptree.

As I write now, it is quite interesting looking back what a different world Lawrence, Christine's dad, lived in and how wealthy he was. I cannot say I had any real awareness of his wealth as I began to spend more time in his company. He simply never mentioned his circumstances. He did however often make statements about his wealth through his actions, one such occasion being a jockeys' charity evening held in Wells.

This event was my first evening suit affair - I don't recall if this was before or after Christine and I were married. You made money in one of two ways - you either bet on a horse or you bought a horse. The race was screened so all participants could watch (the races were often from Hong Kong, so no one knew who was going to win). The winning horse paid out either on bets you had placed or on horses you had purchased. Each race there were maybe up to fifteen horses. Lawrence of course purchased, Christine and I simply bet. In the purchase pot it was entirely possible to gather in excess of £20,000 a race. Those that purchased horses took 50% of the pot should their horse win.

The whole event was held up until Lawrence (the biggest spender of the night by far) and his party of 20 arrived. We sat at the centre table, beneath which were boxes of chilled champagne. When the bidding started, Lawrence paid several thousand pounds for the first horse, and over the evening he spent £9000 on buying horses. At around the same time, our first house cost £9700. I don't think he won a penny, and how much the champagne cost I would hate to say. Christine and I spent about ten pounds.

As I said before, Lawrence never mentioned his wealth, except to arrive in a brand new Rolls Royce. He was the number one man that evening among many of the upper crust of the local racing fraternity.

Lawrence owned four racehorses and had a live-in stable lad who was to later to marry Christine's sister Lol. He also owned the local butcher's shop at Bishop Sutton and one of only two abattoirs in the country that was licensed to slaughter horses, which were exported in the main to Holland and Belgium for human consumption. Much of the wealth came from this activity. As business boomed a new Rolls Royce was purchased every year and an outdoor swimming pool was built, heated all year round. In winter steam could be seen rising from the pool. He was a millionaire several times over. Some said he was not a good businessman, but somehow I doubt this. He was a self-made man and millionaires were not common in the seventies.

Back to the wedding. We set a date in December. Being a Roman Catholic and wanting to get married in church, I had to ask Father Garrigan's permission to marry a non-Catholic, and Christine and I had to make three visits to Father Garrigan to ensure Christine would understand and be prepared to bring the children up in the Catholic faith.

Father Garrigan loved a whisky, and on two occasions when we took along a bottle his eyes sparkled and I can still hear his Irish brogue even now - "by Jasus Michael, I shall enjoy that shortly". I had known him all my life, and some Sunday mornings he would arrive at mass with a black eye where he had fallen the previous night from a little too much whisky. The Mass on these Sundays rarely lasted twenty minutes and most Sundays it was an hour.

The wedding went well, except that when I was repeating the vows, I said "I take thee Christine John Potter", John being Christine's brother, who sadly died in his early thirties. Christine's middle name was Jean. Our reception was in one of the finest hotels of its day, yet I had literally no money. I borrowed the £44 for my three-piece wedding suit, the equivalent today of probably £500, from my dad, who ultimately told me to have it as a wedding present. All our furniture and our cooker had been bought on hire purchase, and I even had to borrow the money for the flowers and bridesmaids' presents. A peculiar start, but not one that bothered me much or seemed out of order. Christine, as I recall, was to sell her car to help fund some of the items for the home. We kept the Spitfire and Christine used the Minivan from work.

Our honeymoon night, would you believe, was spent at the mother-in-law's. We affectionately knew her as Mrs P. We moved into a two-bedroom council bungalow newly built at Compton Martin, just 400 yards from where Mum and Dad lived, and stayed there for about two and a half years.

In those first few weeks of our marriage Christine missed her mother quite a lot. She was only 19 years old and we spent quite a bit of time at Mrs P's. We were of course both working. I was nearly always home first, and it seemed natural for me to start cooking the evening meal on the new cooker. I remember that first meal, steak, chips and peas - simple but the execution of the meal was anything but. We had been given a deep-fry chip pan as one of our wedding presents and it was heating away beautifully when I decided it would be nice to have a couple of tomatoes with the meal. All was going very well, but as I tipped the home-made chips into the pan, there was a massive hiss as the rather wet chips hit the oil. The fat instantly caught fire and exploded over the edge of the pan, flames leaping high into the air. I rushed to the sink and soaked the towel in water, but the flames and fat seemed to be everywhere. I rushed back to the cooker, laid the wet towel over the pan and cooker and without waiting picked up the chip pan and dashed outside with it. Fortunately the wet towel I had wrapped around the very hot pan, including the handle, prevented any personal damage. Shaken but not stirred, I cleaned up and finished cooking the dinner. I did not tell Christine what had happened until three weeks later.

The dairy where I had started my working life eleven years previously, in 1962, was closing down, being too small to meet the needs of the seventies economy. I was offered a supervisory role in Swansea, but Swansea seemed like the end of the world at the time, especially as we had not long been married, so I took my redundancy. It was enough to buy a near-new Ford Capri with a fantastic engine, built on a day when everyone at the car factory worked in perfect harmony. Back in those days, so the story went, if you got a Friday-built car you got a load of trouble, but this car was never any trouble. It used not a drop of oil, started first time every time and went like the wind.

I was back in work one week after being made redundant, but I had returned to the ranks. Although my job title was pasteurizer, in truth I was not much more than a machine-minder. It was a lazy kind of job, monitoring plant operations mostly from a chair. Boredom was available by the bucket.

A year after joining the Co-Op from Unigate, I

became the Shop Steward at the Whitby Road Plant in Brislington. I did lead a one-day strike and was able to negotiate one or two good pay deals for the lads.

In between times Christine and I had a fantastic holiday in Jersey, making friends with two young couples in Nottingham who we visited after the holidays. We also had an adventurous holiday in Cornwall camping. We borrowed a tent from our friends Liz and Ken Wheeler and had only been there a day when an unfortunate series of events took place. We had taken two small gas burners. One was lit for cooking breakfast when I decided to light the second one to make drinks. As I tried to screw the canister into the burner, gas leaked from it and a couple of seconds later the gas was ignited by the flames of the other burner. I was holding the burner between my legs, and the flames were so intense that they melted my trousers and removed every hair on my legs. The base of the tent was now also melting and oxygen depletion was almost total, so we both got out as quick as we could. Christine had the presence of mind to go and get a fire extinguisher, and only the floor of the tent was burnt.

Looking down at my trousers I realized what a lucky escape I had had. My trousers were melted and my legs covered in singed hairs, but all other parts were intact and unharmed. We spent the rest of the week with a couple of friends, Pete and Jackie, who were holidaying in a caravan not far from our camp site.

Somewhere between 1974 and 1975 we bought

Forge House, the first house we had owned. It was about half a mile from Mrs P's house, on the main road between Clutton and Temple Cloud. The purchase was somewhat difficult and was done at auction, Forge House being the last lot to be sold on the evening.

Lawrence was to do the bidding for us and had agreed to pay the deposit of 10%, thus providing a bridge until we were able to raise a mortgage - at least that was the theory. We anticipated a price of around £6,750 and a 90% mortgage. Our planning was not perfect and our estimations even less so.

The auction was at the Bear and Swan, Chew Magna. It began with the first bid at £4700 and rose in bids of £500, reaching £7200 relatively quickly. Lawrence came in at £6700 and continued to bid up to £8200. Bids were now slowing. Lawrence looked towards us, as we had indicated that £8000 was our absolute limit, and I nodded to continue bidding. There were five more bids, one at £500 more and four of £250. Lawrence was buying now regardless of what we thought, and his last bid took the house at a final cost of £9700.

The previous owners looked well satisfied, and shook our hands and bought us drink. Christine and I left that evening well pleased, but a bit shocked at the price we did not actually have a mortgage in place and were soon to learn that this would be very difficult. Eventually we were offered a 70% mortgage, meaning we would have to find £2910. We had precisely £992. Not only were we short of the deposit, we would not receive the funds from the building society for at least six weeks. The rules of auction said we had thirty days to pay or forfeit the deposit Lawrence had paid.

We took our building society passbook to see a mortgage broker, who was helpful but not hopeful he could sort it out in the time span available.

Three weeks had elapsed and the broker was no further forward. Christine explained to her dad what was happening and his reaction was simple - King Miles (the auctioneers) will not be saying Lawrence Potter cannot pay his bills, and he paid for the house the next day. The broker, who was based in Bristol, was stunned that Christine's dad could simply pay outright. We were saved. A mortgage was agreed between Lawrence and us at 1½% below the market rate, which was at that time 11% (any lower would have looked like a gift, our solicitor said). We paid the mortgage for about four months before Lawrence said the house was ours. Unfortunately he never gave us the deeds, which was to be a problem later. The house was paid for by one of the Dutch traders who bought horses from Lawrence, some form of tax fiddle or simply the hiding of a gift I really don't know, but it got us out of a pretty big mess.

Lawrence also bought John's, Michael's and Lol's houses, but not Joan's. Upon his death, Maggie, Lawrence's second wife, handed Lol her deeds. John had received his immediately after the purchase of his house, but Maggie refused to hand over the deeds to our house or Michael's. Ultimately these houses were paid for by trust deposits equal to the value of the house purchases, the deposits being made by myself and Michael – but more about this later.

We never really had any money, but on one occasion Christine thought she had spotted an opportunity to make some money on a Mk 1 Ford Cortina which was up for sale for £75. The big ends had gone (shell bearings in the crankshaft) and the car rattled like a box of bolts. Christine, convinced I could sort it out, bought the car, and I bought a Haynes manual to help me with the replacement of the bearings. The engine had to come out, yet my nearest previous experience had been replacing a head gasket.

The car was positioned over the pit in Mrs P's garage and I borrowed a hoist, I believe from Martin Cole, a fellow badminton player, and set about the task. Cars in the seventies were fairly basic compared to today's models and the task of removing the engine and stripping it down and putting it back together was not so difficult. I remember improvising with a home-made piston ring compressor made from a baked bean can sliced down the middle, which allowed me to squeeze the piston rings around the piston and drop them back into the engine block. The job took me about four weeks, mostly weekends. Having paid £75 for the car and £40 for parts, we sold the car for £135. You can do the sums, but we were not going to get rich down this route. However some valuable new knowledge and skills had been gained. I recall somewhere around this period

Mrs P having her roof retiled and I volunteered to replace the soffit boards and fit a new chimney pot. I was not good at heights, so Jonathan, my brother-in-law, volunteered to carry it up the roof, then I would crawl up to cement it on. The day before I had blackened Mrs P's sitting room in removing the old chimney pot. Unable to move freely up and down the roof, I simply broke it off and let it go down the chimney. It crashed all the way down, bringing clouds of soot into the sitting room. Incidentally Jonathan got stuck halfway up the roof with the chimney pot, and I had to take it off him.

# Three jobs in a day

The house sorted and behind us, Mrs P's roof completed and our venture into wheeler dealing over, opportunities opened up at work. The Regional General Manager of the South Western Co-Operative Society was keen on management development training, and given my previous background in training (I had a couple of National Dairy Diplomas) and the fact that someone from the production unit was needed to make up a team of eight managers, I was off and running with my management career. It is worth noting at this time the Co-op was bigger than the combined shopping fraternity of Sainsbury's, Tesco's and Marks and Spencers put together so the opportunity was significant.

Four junior managers were paired with four senior managers. My senior manager was the Regional Transport Manager and our project was cost reduction,

Whitby Road Production Plant (Dairy). In truth of course I was not a manager and my lack of knowledge was to frequently embarrass me, for example when everyone talked glibly about GP, NP, growth targets, white goods and brown goods I simply did not understand. But I learned to swallow my pride and ask. Some sessions were painfully slow as a result, but there was recognition of my need to catch up and a degree of patience.

Much went on that was not all learning and the project driven by the Regional Butchery Manager and his Junior Manager, who was Assistant Training Officer, went completely off the rails when they had a raging affair, both eventually losing their jobs. The Dairy Cost Reduction Project did go well, with major cost savings and specific hygiene measures being identified and embraced within our final submission. I had researched all the costs, drafted all the operational changes and applied some radical thoughts to the weekly operating cycle. The latter had been fought with major lobbying by some of the mainstream dairy management. My senior mentor was a tense and highly-strung guy who admitted he kept a note pad and pen on his bedroom table just in case he woke and had a really good thought. He suggested I do the same. I did not, but to be quite frank, I often wished over the years that I had.

At the close of the management Development project I had learned much. I was given a new Job as Production Co-ordinator and a £5000 salary, but the job lasted two hours, with the workforce going on strike the moment I walked into the dairy at Whitby Road. You have to remember I had been their shop Steward before stepping across the line. After several hours of debate it was decided that my position and the company's were not tenable, and I was appointed to a new role of Transport Manager on the same salary. I could tell this had a zero chance of lasting and at four o'clock I approached the Regional Transport Manager and suggested that he speak to his boss, the South West's Regional General Manager, and put me forward for the now vacant Assistant Training Manager's role. He reacted with considerable favour, only confirming my earlier thoughts that he had not wanted me in the role of Transport Manager, nor for that matter had any of his team - too many noses out of joint, and to be perfectly honest the job had absolutely no appeal to me.

So at 5.45 that afternoon I had my third job of the day as Assistant Training Manager. I was playing in a badminton match that evening for Chew Magna and I recall the club captain asking me what my job was. Of course, I was able to say "Well today I have had three jobs, Richard". Richard had a dry sense of humour and responded with, "Seems I picked a good day to ask you Mike". Some years later Richard's son was to work for me as a planner at Courages.

Christine and I were both playing badminton by now (Christine was a really good player, having twice been a finalist in our inter-club tournament). We had joined a club of beginners at Ubley, all about our age, and it was not long before we had entered a team into the North Somerset Badminton League. We named our team Bell-Ubley as there was already an Ubley Badminton club playing at the hall and in the North Somerset league. Although Christine and I played as a pair in mixed doubles, that came to an end one evening when we had a right falling out. It was entirely my fault, but Christine was so mad as we were leaving the court that she threw her racket with great force towards the back of the stage, where those not playing were sitting. It hit Kenny Mitchell, causing a three-inch burn mark down the side of his neck. We did not play as a pair again.

Badminton was probably my best sport, and at Bell-Ubley I won several mixed doubles cups. Once a year we invited other clubs, local rivals like Dundry, Bishopworth and of course the original Ubley Badminton club, to play in an American Handicap Cup Competition, which I organised and ran. The event was played over two weeks (six nights in reality, with the finals being played on the last evening with the last game often concluding at two in the morning). The better player pairings started on a minus score, with others beginning on a positive score according to their skills level. In the two mixed tournaments I won we started with minus twenty. My partner was Elaine Small from Bishop Sutton.

In my first three years of playing league badminton (all for Chew Magna) I did not lose a single mixed doubles rubber (sorry about the boast). The Bell-Ubley club had by now about 26 members. Two really good teams among the players were Lol and Jonathan, my sister and brother-in-law. Jonathan was a pretty good player and Lol was quite good, playing in the Bell-Ubley second team.

Back at work my new job was going reasonably well. I had completed my induction, which was quite varied and sometimes a bit of a shock. The Co-op was a business that operated in many fields, including a very large funeral service provision across Bristol and adjacent suburbs. It was obligatory for new training guys to take a tour of the mortuary at a slow and detailed pace. Even now I recall the shock of seeing a one-year-old child, head platted from the autopsy investigation. I was taken to the embalming room, empty thank heavens, and then to the presentation rooms, where the deceased lay for visits by their relatives. In the first lay a man who was dressed immaculately in a suit and tie and lay in his coffin with almost a smile. He had tight curly hair and a suntanned complexion and looked completely at peace. In the next was a 33-year-old man who had drowned during an epileptic fit. I was shown how access had been made in his head for the autopsy, the offending hole filled with wax and perfect make-up applied to camouflage the wax and the hole. The mortician explained this in detail and with genuine professional pride.

I had never seen a dead person until that moment

and of course the tour was designed to shock. It did so, but I did not faint or become queasy as many had before, though I still see those dead faces today, even as I write these memoirs.

Next I was put in charge of a management development program for junior managers across all functions. I watched some early internal politics on this one, with the Regional Grocery Manager in particular distancing himself from the exercise and putting his number two forward as the front man. Others were playing ball even though they believed the project doomed to failure. Interestingly, Duncan Campbell, head of the Non-Food Division, who was a play-along doubter, spent quite a bit of time with me assessing how best to accommodate the programme. He played his part well with the development scheme and with the Regional General Manager who had instigated the programme and was very much its sponsor.

A year later the head of the Non-Food Division became Regional General manager South Wales, not because he went along with the scheme but because he knew how to play the game. Well that's what I thought.

The process of learning my job was speeding up, and I recall simply enjoying every new experience, one of which was recruiting for and supporting the training programmes for the opening of a new Co-operative superstore at Hartcliffe (now Morrisons). On the first day of interviews, some 600 plus people turned up for an interview. I had never conducted an interview and had no training. There was a team of eight sitting in four rooms interviewing simultaneously. Those individuals of apparent quality were passed to a second interview and possible job offer. Ours lasted a maximum of ten minutes and was a fact and filter process (name, age, address, previous experience). I simply followed the flow of interview paper and copied the Assistant Personnel Manager's approach, as he was interviewing in the same room. We were unable to complete the interviewing of all those who had attended, despite having started at 9 am and concluding at 6 pm. We invited those who had not gone through the filter interview to return the following day, which they did, along with another hundred people. Our process at the filter and extended interview stage had become highly selective, and on day three it became obvious that we had been too selective.

I recall on Day Two a young girl who was so nervous and had such a stammer that it was five minutes before I got her name. I felt such a pig when I could not pass her on to the second stage. Just over a week later we had to run some additional interviews, which were done at our local shop in Symes Avenue, Hartcliffe, and I remember being pinned against the counter by a woman in her late thirties who promised me a real good time should she be successful with her job application. She was not.

I recall for the first time having to address a very large number of people, some one hundred successful recruits. Most of them were women. The address was very formal, outlining pay arrangements, duty hours, acceptable dress, holiday arrangements, etc, and it was quite daunting first time out, but another new experience under my belt.

Somewhere in the middle of this new career we were getting Forge House together. The weather in 1975 and 1976 was fabulous and I recall one tremendously hot day when we went to Lawrence's for a drink, barbecue and a swim. All the family were there and some of his friends. It was very hot, so I went into the pool I could not swim that well, in fact hardly at all, and while I was floating across the deep end one of the kids jumped on me. I knew as I came up for the second time that I was drowning. The air had gone from my lungs and it was so difficult to take in enough air as you surfaced and then sank again. I panicked, and when I went down for the third time the only thing I could do was hold my arm above the water and kick like mad trying to resurface, but to no avail. Joan, Christine's third sister and one of the triplets, spotted I was in trouble and took my hand and pulled me to the surface, saving my life. I was only two feet from the side of the pool and probably no more than a foot and half from the bottom, but had she not grabbed my hand it would have been curtains.

I recall one or two people saying I looked rather pale. It was a while before I got into the pool again. Today I doubt Joan or anyone else who was present will remember, but I do. It was an awful feeling, and I felt unbelievable relief as she gripped my hand.

Time seemed to move quickly across the seventies - married, house bought and before I knew it Christine was pregnant, and I was out of a job for the second time. We had been trying for months for a child. In the end she used some form of fertility aid and pregnancy was achieved in a very short time.

The news at work was less good. The top man at the Co-op had moved on, frustrated by too many committees. He had always given me support, but now a new RGM was in situ. He was a year younger than me, brash and unnecessarily dismissive of all that had gone before. Within two weeks he had declared my job redundant. My boss offered to take redundancy too, thus allowing me to step into his job, but Howard Prudhoe, the Regional Personnel Manager and the man to whom I would report, was not a fan of mine. He had not forgotten my arrogance as a shop Steward, when I had treated him as my equal, nor my more recent criticism of his personnel records and systems, I lost my job.

For those reading this story today and making their way along the managerial path, you might just consider the merits or otherwise of uncensored freedom of expression, for some day it might compromise your future. My forthright approach was of no help this time around. I was never sensitive to the necessity of diplomacy, often believing it was for those who did not believe in their own opinions. Moreover the internal politics of companies often escaped me. Honesty on the other hand I was comfortable with, but today unedited honesty had cost me my job, or at the very least it had helped. The loss of your job is a body blow at the best of times, and the timing is rarely good. With Christine having to give up work shortly, money soon became very tight.

Christine was a very active person, and while she had given up working at the butchery shop and was seven months pregnant she undertook a major body repair and repaint job on her brother-in-law's Mk 2 Cortina, brother-in-law being Richard Spear. It kept her busy, for she simply could not stand being idle. Meanwhile, I collected my £49.50 a week from the dole office (benefits office/job centre) and by the time I had found a job we were well and truly in debt and remained so for many years.

Three months before becoming redundant, during the course of Christine's pregnancy, I had attended the Lancastrian School of management in Carnforth, with two six-week stints at the School of management and a three month project in the workplace. I obtained a Training Officer's Certificate a qualification that was recognized nationally and allowed me to issue Instructor Training Certificates to individuals that attended courses I ran. This certificate was to be my passport to a job, along with a stroke of luck. Before I could pursue employment with vigour, another important event was about to take place.

It was a Wednesday evening early in April and we had just arrived home from table skittles when Christine suggested it might be best to head for Bristol Maternity Hospital, as there were distinct stirrings. We had at the time been suffering from one or two little mice problems, and I said I wanted to set the traps before we set off, as the blighters had already gnawed through electrical wires in the loft. This sorted we were off to the hospital - it was probably about midnight or just after. The birth seemed to take forever, but Christine took only oxygen. The contractions were increasing, but no sign yet of a baby, so at about half past five I set off for a bar of chocolate, a walk and a cigarette.

On my return my firstborn was arriving, and in minutes we had our daughter. As soon as she was in the midwife's arms Christine asked if she was normal. I don't know why, but she wanted to be sure that all her fingers, toes, etc were present and formed as they should be, and of course they were. We were both immensely proud and overjoyed. Christine was quick to name her Kirstie. I recall in those early days taking Kirstie in a carrycot just laid on the back seat of the car to my mother's.

Kirstie was a mite bad-tempered as a baby, and by the time she was two and a half she could raise her voice very loudly, on one occasion frightening her cousin Simon, my sister's boy with such a loud 'don't touch' that he burst into tears. Simon was six weeks younger than Kirstie.

I was of course still out of work. and I decided that becoming a member of The Institute of Training, a professional body that subsequently merged with the Institute of Personnel, I would have a far better chance of getting a job. I had managed just two interviews in two months and was successful at neither, having written to some 25 companies including Courage Limited. I discovered that the Membership Secretary of the Institute of Training for the South West worked for Courage in the role of Training Manager, and I rang her to make an appointment reference my application. The Courage Western Offices at the time were based in Bedminster in the old Wills Buildings (now Asda), which were then owned by the Imperial Tobacco Company. The offices were adjacent to the old tobacco factory, which had long been moved to Whitchurch. The Training Manager's office was on the top floor and top notch in style. The walls were of oak panelling, a number of quality portraits hung from the wall and to one side was a hexagonal oak conference table. The chairs would have graced the dining room of any well-to-do family. In less than four years' time this would be my office, but not before I could reignite my management career. I would have to start back at basement level.

The Training Manager, whose name was Audrey, suggested we go to a local pub on the river for lunch, and suggested we use my car. At the time I had a smart Triumph 2000 and had valeted it that morning, creating a good impression. We went through the application process for Institute of Training membership over a sandwich and a beer. It was I thought a rather in-depth enquiry about what I had done previously and where I had qualified, but what the hell, I had all day and the membership of the Institute of Training was important to me. Audrey looked at me a little oddly and said "Would you be interested in joining me at Courage? We have a vacancy for a training assistant. But I was slow to respond and the hesitation was taken as disinterest.

I explained that it was a staff job, not a management role, and the salary was 30% less than I had been getting, but ultimately a job was a job and Christine and I needed some money as we were quickly falling further into debt. I attended two more interviews before being appointed.

The early months were quite interesting, as I participated in both managed house and tenanted pub management training, each being a five-day course for people new to the pub scene (the latter often put large amounts of their own money into the venture). During these courses Keith, the Retail Training Manager (RTM) had the most fabulous lunches prepared, intended to demonstrate what could be done back at their pubs. He frequently filled his doggy bag with half a salmon, beautifully smoked turkey, superbly made salads and many other goodies. Much of my participation was to provide training in interviewing techniques and pub staff training techniques and the keeping of training records. The job also included setting up interviews, from the point of drawing up and advertising the vacancies to selection and taking up references.

After six months I was seconded to the role of Tenanted Sales Manager. I knew very little about the actual pub operations except for what I had gleaned from the training courses. However, I achieved acclaim for the high ratio of successful debt collection, and interestingly, out of the blue, my staff grading was improved and I received an £800 increase, although I was still well short of my previous salary.

There were some genuine bonuses to this secondment, temporarily a company car, invitations to some wonderful trade dinners and occasionally the inebriated conclusion to a tenanted pub visit where either the tenant wanted a favour, was particularly sociable or had been on one of my courses. Such occasions often occurred when the visit coincided with closing time and we sat and relaxed over too many beers. On such occasions I had to ring the office to get someone to collect me, leaving the car at the pub and picking it up the next day. As I was still in Personnel my chauffeur was invariably Harry Cooper, our personnel stats clerk, I couldn't let the trade lads know I could not hold my beer.

After five months it was back to training. I was going to miss the car and the social benefits, and this time it was industrial training, not pub training. The main feature was the writing of three operating manuals for new plant that had been installed, to be used as training manuals for all new entrants. Then came another secondment to Industrial Relations, from which I did not return to training. The initial role was to write some 30-odd 'Craft-Affiliated Job Descriptions.

This secondment proved a big opportunity. I met a wonderfully gifted wordsmith, Bob Harle, who was a personnel consultant. He helped me tremendously, not only with the writing of job descriptions but with my managerial progress in the company. The secondment was a success and I was promoted to management – it was the lowest grade, but at last I had recovered (and added to) to my previous salary at the Co-op. It had taken nearly eighteen months, and it would take a little longer still to be out of debt.

This period of my employment was a big learning curve and my job was affected by the major Trade Union of the day, The Transport and General Workers Union. Even though we had seen the last of the Trade Unions all powerful era of the seventies, unions' power at industrial level was still very strong. All Courage sites had closed shop agreements, no union membership, no job. The workforce, particularly at Avonmouth, was very active with regards to pursuing their rights and laced with ex-dockers, mostly dickheads of the first order who would go on strike at the first opportunity. For instance if there was no tea break man to relieve the operatives on the line when the bottling line started up, they would not begin work, even though there were enough operatives to man every workstation. Through the seventies and much of the early eighties Britain's workforce almost had parity with their companies' bosses and owners. They could withdraw their labour without fear of being sacked. For me today's employment legislation is loaded too heavily in favour of the employer and provides for unfair exploitation of labour. In the seventies and early eighties the opposite was true. It is difficult to keep the pendulum in the middle.

I was lucky to have worked when I did, as the need for persuading a workforce to change the way they worked required much more than a simple legislative override which today has seen employee rights ever more eroded. You needed imagination to understand how the workforce ticked and be able to spot the improbable possibilities of success when others saw no possibility.

Today, I often witness the thoughtless actions of management and in particular politicians and the devastation their decisions cause to the common people of the UK. Maggie Thatcher plundered, pillaged and raped our heavy industry in pursuit of her destruction of Trade Unions. Blair copied her privatisation policies and compromised nearly all Labour's social principles in order to be electable and stay in power. Sadly I fear a Great Britain of minor importance in the not-too-distant future – sorry, I'm off on one again. My own background is steeped in socialism, where equality is sought and should be available for all. I have no room for the plastic imitators or those that have marauded as New Labour and so called socialists since the late 80s.

Back with my story. Courage was a very traditional company steeped in history and modelled accordingly. When I joined in 1979 there was a Senior management and directors' dining room, management dining room, staff and foremen dining room and hourly-paid employees' dining hall. When addressing someone of director status, Mr was still necessary. Lunch for directors began at 12 and finished at 3.30, and many were so inebriated that it was impossible to have any kind of sensible of conversation post lunch - not some days, but every day. At the breweries, senior management went into the sample room, where beers were kept for tasting purposes, every Friday, coming out just in time to start the weekend break.

When I arrived, all sites were wet; when I left, they were all dry (I should explain that in the seventies all brewing sites/offices were wet, i.e. allowed alcohol to be consumed on site, and in the factories beer was served with breakfast. Lunches at all levels had also changed. Now a sandwich sufficed, often eaten without a break for lunch, and only the stuffed shirts of the Scottish Board of directors continued to exhibit such dining room snobbery. No doubt our banking moguls still do.

Things were moving fast at Courage. I was learning the art of negotiating and discovering that I had a natural flare and ability to pick my way through the debates, hostile arguments and sometimes childlike tantrums of the shop Stewards and employees. What was more, I really enjoyed the whole thing.

My next big break came with the merging of all of the Courage Western based sites into one single bargaining unit. This simply meant that wherever you worked, be it one of the breweries, Distribution, Maltings, as a craftsmen, driver, warehouseman or horse groom, your terms and conditions would be covered under a single agreement negotiated between company and Trade Union, covering the geographical area of the bargaining unit. There were four such units within Courage: Courage Western, Courage Eastern, Central and John Smiths. In order to achieve the bargaining merger, all job descriptions would have to be written in a common format and then evaluated, and this was my job for the next six months. Would you believe it, I was given a promotion to Personnel Manager in order to give relevant status. Now I had a decent salary - not exciting, but decent.

I managed to write 68 job descriptions to the satisfaction of some 36 shop Stewards with only one dissenter, and the policing committee of management and Stewards signed the JD on his behalf (the dissenter was an articulated lorry driver whose vocabulary extended only to 'no'). Twelve managers and 48 hourly-paid employees turned out on a Saturday to do the judging. The exercise was based on a "pairs comparison" system - every job was compared with every other job. The judges simply scored 2 for the bigger job and 0 for the lesser. Where the jobs were considered equal, a posting of 1/1 was given. This latter option was discouraged as it could lead to large blocks of jobs being rated the same and have an impact on the coefficient of agreement, important in establishing the legitimacy of the pairs comparison process. The objective was to achieve an 85% coefficient of agreement, and ultimately we hit 87%.

To keep everyone on their toes all judges had been threatened with a 12-member panel of assessors who would interrogate their every decision, particularly where it was blatantly obviously wrong, ie porter v surgeon, where the porter had been given the 2/0 decision as had happened in one of the training sessions. Moreover I had told the management and employees that such blatant errors would be published for all employees to see. It worked perfectly. There were no discernible errors and concerned employees - and indeed managers - were at pains to point out any difficult decisions they had made. Leaving modesty aside for a moment, the whole exercise was such a success that I receive a second promotion in less than a year and with it a company car. I was now Industrial Relations Manager for Courage Western, covering Devon and Cornwall, Bristol, Gloucester and South Wales.

★ ★ ★ ★ ★

At home a new arrival had joined us, namely Scott. We were both very pleased to have a boy and girl. Kirstie was just about sleeping at night after I had spent many an evening on the kitchen floor with her so her mum could get some sleep. Scott I recall got the rough end of the stick because of Kirstie's poor sleeping habits, and was left to cry for quite a while until at last he went to bed without any trouble at all. Then suddenly James was born. His temperature gave some concern, being marginally below 36 degrees, but he did arrive very quickly, within forty minutes of getting to the hospital.

By the time Kirstie was four I was already into my homespun bedtime stories. Scott often listened but usually fell asleep halfway through. James of course was too young, but he went to bed with little or no trouble right from the start, sucking his thumb for comfort. Mind you I don't think he stopped until he was eleven.

One story I still recall very easily. It was about Mr and Mrs Yellow, who lived in a yellow house with a yellow mouse. One night we had live participation. Thank god it had not happened the previous night, as it had been a story about the elephant of Compton Martin woods. Kirstie, I noticed, was wide awake and wide eyed, but Scott was already dozing. She turned to me and said, "Dad, is that the mouse? And sure enough there scuttling across the floor was a live mouse. "Yes, that's the one" I said, lifting my feet onto the chair rungs. Kirstie said "It's brown." "Yes" I said, "It's wearing its winter coat."

The mouse disappeared into the wardrobe and I finished the story just as Kirstie fell asleep.

In truth I never did enough with the children. I made Kirstie a shop when she was four and we walked from Mrs P's house to ours with it on a very cold day. Her hands were blue by the time we got home. Kirstie would simply not let go of the shop, which was made mostly from pallet wood, and insisted on walking the half mile up the road, helping me carry the shop from Mrs P's and then wishing to play shops the moment we got home.

When James was three I made him a farmyard with barns and pens, gates etc as a Christmas present. I think he enjoyed it. Scott and I did a bit of fishing together. Scott had to show me what to do, but I do remember his joy when he caught his first fish and his anguish and pain when I hooked his hand. The hook being barbed, it took an age to extract. Scott was about ten and I remember a single tear as I finally extracted the hook, Scott suggested he was a baby. "Not at all, son", I recall saying.

Work consumed so much of my time and energy that I had little time left for the kids. We did have one or two enjoyable holidays and one or two good day trips out as a family. Now, however, I am able to spend some good quality time with all my grandchildren, through their lovable years when they say and do things that bring you great joy.

This episode of my life is difficult to talk about. When James was still very much a baby, Christine developed a continuous headache. The doctor told her it was exhaustion from childbirth and having three children so young. That diagnosis was hopelessly wrong, so much so that when he later attempted to justify his mistake, I dismissed his utterances. I write this entry with the anguish of the loss of Christine a loss burned upon my mind, without wishing to ignite the memory of the pain, loneliness and heartache that exploded upon me. So my apologies if this entry is perhaps more brief that one would expect.

We had enjoyed a very good marriage and had three wonderful children. We loved, laughed and cried together, and life was looking good. Now I find myself reading condolence letters and cards, tears pouring down my cheeks. The children sit around me. Scott reaches out to say "Don't cry Dad", and I cannot tell them their mother is dead. Instead I tell them she has gone to heaven.

The funeral arrived so quickly. I rode in the hearse with Christine to the church at Clutton, our last journey together. No arrangements had been made for after the funeral. I could not cope with people at this moment - it was as much as I could bear to have the family around me. The flowers stretched from the entrance gate forever down both sides of the church path and right up to the doors. When everyone had gone home I went back to the churchyard to say goodbye and promise Christine once again that I would take care of the children forever, just as I had in the hospital.

The weeks and months that follow were filled with

hurt and emptiness. Mrs P was helpful and Joan Spear, my sister-in-law, was so very supportive. I found I could talk to her.

The children kept me upright. They were my sole focus. Many people offered their condolences, and I simply said thank you. I never engaged in conversation; the pain penetrated every part of me. I could not talk to the children, as the memories and the loss were locked away. When Kirstie went back to school the other children told her with the brutal honesty of childhood that her mum was dead, and she came home and asked me if it was true. "I didn't know, Dad" she said. I had of course told her that her mum had gone to heaven. Now I simply said "Yes, that is true".

Christmas was difficult. When I asked the children if they were enjoying themselves Kirstie said "Yes Dad, but it would be nicer with Mum here".

We did not speak of Mum for many years after this. Was that right? Probably not, but you cope with life as you cope with life, and I had no strength to manage it any other way.

I have only visited the grave once, upon the loss of Christine's mum. Now I am able to remember without pain, but never without sadness. Occasionally when the grandchildren are playing I think how proud Christine would be of them. You see time does heal, pain is lessened and life begins to return to normal. There were many lonely nights, but the children were present to give comfort. I hated being without them, and although Mrs

P liked to take them home with her it was something I dreaded. For those reading this now there is no more I can say, except to recall a fleeting moment when I sat on the children's swing at Forge House and felt Christine's hand on my shoulder. Whether she was saying "goodbye" or "you'll be all right" I don't know, but my shock was so great. The moment came and went in less than a few seconds, but I will remember it always.

I had now to go back to work, and the Safety Officer whisked me off to Bath Street Brewery, where everyone was very kind. The next day we went to Plymouth Brewery.

Soon it was becoming apparent that Mrs P was struggling. The children were young and needed much attention, and they were clearly tiring her out. The long search for someone to help look after the children began. It is difficult to express the exhaustion, pain and grief that came with this process.

Many those I spoke with had too much baggage, like the woman who wanted to bring four dogs. Another wanted an entertainment allowance. I learned later she was an alcoholic and I guess wanted the allowance for her addiction. Most, like me had two or more children, but many of them had children of the world, children looking more like representatives of the United Nations - one Indian, another European and sometimes a West Indian. The more I looked, the more desperate it became. Most were young enough to be my daughter. Through these dark times it was my children who kept me upright.

In the evenings, weekends and holidays, I cared for the children and we enjoyed time together. Poor old James caught chicken pox and the poor little blighter was covered from head to foot in some of the most savage spots you will ever see, so changing his nappy was a very delicate matter. Then he fell over with a pencil in his hand which promptly stuck in his face, causing heavy bleeding. I almost fainted when I saw the blood and how close the pencil had gone to his eye. Then just to top it off, when I was bathing all three together, James slipped through my hands and dived head first into the water. He literally came up blowing bubbles before going into a raging squall.

Scott and Kirstie fared a little better, though Scott had to have a wart cut from his finger, which the doctor removed simply by squeezing his finger and cutting. Kirstie was favoured with a beautiful teddy bear from the local Post Office and many new dresses, and she was allowed to drive my company car around the fields near a camp site where we had taken a break with Mrs P.

I was doing my own washing at this time and remember on one occasion putting my suit trousers in the washing machine as grease had gone all over one of the legs. I had bought the suit only a few weeks previously. On taking them from the machine, I found that the legs were now four inches shorter than before. In a moment of stupidity, I desperately attempted to stretch them before banishing them to the dustbin.

Life can be a bugger, but sometimes luck runs your

way, and Lorraine certainly ran my way. Lorraine, whose kids had grown up, was looking once again to be part of a family, having moved to Wells to stay with her Uncle Tommy, a cracking fellow. It was good to have someone to talk to, to help with the children and to be home when I returned from work, for despite being surrounded by people I was immensely lonely, and I could feel the loneliness eating into me. Lorraine became my wife in less than a year, and a new chapter began.

# CHAPTER FOUR

# The brewery business

At work I was catching up with my promotions. Through the job evaluation exercise, I had lifted my profile with management across the West and South Wales, and among the Trade Union hierarchy, namely the union professionals. These guys were on a par with management, employed by the various Trade Unions, all with company cars, to look after their members' interests and negotiate the best deals possible for those members. The Transport and General Workers Union had some 2.5 million members at this time. This period of just over a year was a difficult time and saw the demise of many of operations. Eventually I was to personally sign some 400 redundancy letters. It was the beginning of the end for small breweries like the one in Plymouth where some of the guys had worked almost their entire lives. The maltings in Oakhill, Somerset, would close. Mega-breweries had been built and ultimately Courage Limited would go, but that was a while off and I had much work and learning yet to do.

By 1986 I had gobbled up control of the industrial relations front in Courage Western and was being offered the role of Employee Relations Manager in Courage Central. The location covered the largest brewery in Europe at Reading and distribution depots at Coventry, Birmingham, Reading, Weybridge (next to the old Brooklands racing track), Southampton, Isle of White, Ludgershall (close to Salisbury plain) and later Northampton and Kettering.

The next six years were to be a trial of endurance, frustration, learning and massive disappointment - the worst working years of my life. My appointment had been made without the support of my new boss, and he was a nasty piece of work. The Production Director appeared semi-demented at times and the Trade Union Convener (chief Shop Steward) had principles which I did not recognise. The main Trade Union official was an extreme left-wing socialist and highly ambitious. I had of course come from an environment where the Trade Union Officials were close working colleagues who I had often dined with, went sailing with and spent pleasurable evenings with while discussing company business. The Employee Relations Director had said to me "You'll be working in a fish bowl Mike", and how bloody right he was.

I had left my spacious oak-panelled office in

Bedminster to find I had no office in Reading and had to use the Library. The guy I was replacing was still in situ, so there was no space for me, and my new boss, Mr Ions, seemed to enjoy this fact. Eventually, two months after I arrived, the Staff Manager retired and his job was being absorbed into mine. I arrived at six on the Monday morning after he had left and took up residence in his office. My new boss was aghast when he arrived at nine to find me in this rather decent office. My secretary was just the other side of the office wall, which was very convenient. My boss even tried to move me out, but became very aware I was not for moving. Ions would though take his revenge through the annual salary review. I had been appointed without being interviewed by him and it was obvious he would not make me welcome. The failure to provide his most senior manager with an office was an early indication of his attitude towards me.

The promotion had been a significant one, a substantial improvement in my pension, healthcare for the entire family, upgrade of company car and other fringe benefits such as share options. The salary had gone up 25%, though it was in reality a very poor salary for the band I now found myself in. When my delightful new boss gave me the lowest possible annual increase I was on 80.2% of the band rate, the band extending from 80% to 120%. Fortunately the Personnel Director, who had appointed me, had been undertaking a salaries anomaly review and rang me at home to tell me that mine would be increased by £2000 pa – better, but not brilliant. It would be many years before my salary would hit the 120% mark and in between thousands of pounds would be lost. It can be costly being the butt of internal politics.

When my boss told me the next morning it was abundantly obvious that he was less than pleased about this intervention. I just had a moment's fun by thanking him and adding "No doubt Colin, you were instrumental in gaining this increase". His face was contorted with hostility.

Settling into this job was very difficult. I was doing a round trip of 180 miles a day to the office, and some weeks I would drive upwards of 1250 miles. I did more miles looking for a house at weekends, and I was getting married very shortly.

Then the staff annual review negotiations went pear-shaped. Hanson PLC had bought Imperial Tobacco, of which Courage Ltd was a part, and reduced the Review Mandate (the amount I had to spend to reach a settlement) at Berkshire/Central. The settlement had always been a carbon copy of the Industrial Settlement in Central, but not this year, and the staff went on strike for the first time in their history. That was on Wednesday. I was getting married on the Saturday and we were going on holiday with the children after the wedding. We had to delay our holiday until I could sort the strike out.

The wedding took place across the road from Forge

House in the Methodist Chapel and the reception was in Clutton Hall. I borrowed one of the company limousines for the wedding and Gerry, my niece's husband, acted as chauffeur, driving Lorraine slowly around the block before arriving back at the chapel. It was a very good day and evening. Lorraine had made a superb wedding cake and her dress was fabulous. There is a video of the wedding which one day we will get round to converting to a DVD. Brian and Bill, Lorraine's boys, both in their twenties, were ushers for the day and became somewhat inebriated during the course of the evening. They jokingly began calling me Dad, but of course their children became my grandchildren and provided me with much fun. Although one should never favour, for whatever reason Bill's son Andrew and I formed a close bond, and during his early years we were very close. Often tears were noticeable on his departure back to Ramsgate.

Andrew's take on life is simple and straightforward. As he got older we walked the dogs together. One day when he was ten or eleven he turned to me and said "Granddad, you're not Dad's dad, are you?"

"No" I said.

"So you're not really my Granddad are you?"

Again I said no. Andrew replied, "Well that's OK Granddad, just thought I would check" and on we walked with the dogs.

The family had increased overnight, as I had inherited three additional children including Lorraine's daughter

Joanne. However they were adults and had their own father. Lorraine and I were to play host to all three, with Bill coming almost every summer. A quiet man, he enjoyed soccer and was highly knowledgeable about cars - in fact managing the repair of them was to become his profession. He followed Grand Prix racing with a particular interest and these were the topics on which we most engaged. His views on politics and what was right for the country were surprisingly not far from mine.

Joanne was also quiet and on her own admission a shy person. She saw less of us simply because of her devotion to her dogs and the difficulty of getting away. Although we are now free to travel wherever we want as our dogs have gone, it is not in my nature to sit and visit for days on end, even hours. I have a restlessness that is always with me. My need to be doing something, planning my next DIY project, preparing the garden for the following year, going to football or simply driving home is part of my make-up.

I recall on one occasion Joanne stayed with us, going to the Lansdown pub in Derry Hill for an evening meal with her and her boyfriend Russell and of course Lorraine. It turned out to be a rather good evening, thanks partly to an uncontrolled bout of flatulence from yours truly. This happened just as there was a lull in conversation and there was no way of hiding our blushes. The best way to deal with it, I thought, was to mention it in non-apologetic terms to our adjacent diners. Turning to the next table, I said

"Sometimes you know food is so unforgiving", and her response in a quintessentially English voice was "Never mind, my father farts at each and every turn of the Sainsbury's shopping aisles". Joanne and Lorraine did not know where to hide and Russell failed to stifle an enormous fit of laughter. The conversation continued for a while and it certainly enlivened our evening. The food was rather good as well, and Russell felt it was probably one of the most entertaining meals he had ever been present at. Bloody nice fellow was Russell, great sense of humour, fine sketcher, sometimes wayward, but there you go.

Brian of course came to live in Wiltshire, in fact he lived with us for a while. We shared some common interests, one in particular being football, and when he finished his globetrotting for Airbus UK via Bristol, Hamburg and Toulouse, he and his family returned to Wiltshire, living at Shaw, and we started watching Swindon Town occasionally. In 2011 we missed very few games. Brian has also fixed up a couple of visits to Arsenal. In 2012 we went the whole hog and bought season tickets.

When Brian moved to Toulouse we visited him, Linda and the family on a couple of occasions. He is a Stress Engineer working for Airbus UK (previously I believe part of British Aerospace). We had some great hospitality and in the garden was a pretty large swimming pool. With such high temperatures the pool is much used.

We also had a couple of moments here and there, one of those being a visit to Carcassonne, a very old fortified French town, south of Toulouse. On the return journey I missed the motorway exit and we ended up in the rush hour traffic of Toulouse, in a French car (so no one gave you any space), driving round and round the city, with James and our grandchildren Elliott and Grace. Eventually I decided we were not going to find our way back to Brian's, which was about five miles outside Toulouse, so I pulled up at the nearest public phone box (still no mobiles then), set up the picnic table and we had an impromptu picnic on the pavement. Lorraine meanwhile rang Brian for help, giving him the street name. Brian arrived about 40 minutes later and we followed him home.

During the visit to Carcassonne I purchased two flintlock pistols - decorative you understand - and on the trip home I was arrested on discovery of the guns and escorted onto the plane by two armed policeman. The guns were handed to the pilot on boarding by the French police and I got them back on landing at Filton.

With Brian and Linda living much closer it is inevitable we now see a lot more of them and we occasionally dine out together to celebrate birthdays, and recently to recognise Brian's promotion to Deputy Chief Engineer at Airbus UK based at Filton in Bristol.

★ ★ ★ ★ ★

As I was saying before when talking about Lorraine's children, we had just got married and now I had a strike to sort. The holiday was booked, but there was no point dumping the family in Devon. Lorraine could not drive so it would be little fun for them. The problems with sorting out the strike were many. First the industrial employees had to be persuaded not to join forces with the staff, and secondly they had to be persuaded to cross the staff picket line. Then I had to find a stopgap solution concerning the reasons for the strike in order to allow a return to work.

The Convener could not stand the Trade Union Officer, so would quite willingly work against him rather than working with me to persuade the industrial employees not to join forces with the staff and in particular to cross the picket line - just what was needed. Arrangements were made for me, staff managers (none of whom spoke to each other), Trade Union official and Convener to address the industrial shop Stewards at the company's local sports ground on the Thursday, two days after the strike had started.

Fortunately the Luggershall staff had picketed their depot during the day and then gone to work in the evening as industrial employees to clean the depot offices. One of the strikers was the Staff Rep, and some of the industrial Stewards accused them openly of double standards. The meeting was a rough affair. The line managers were sitting on the stage. None spoke, and at one point one of the Stewards accused me of lying. I leapt from the stage, wagging my finger with great fury at the Steward. The room fell silent. The Steward withdrew his accusation and we moved on.

Brian Revell, the Trade Union Official, was next to address them. He represented both hourly paid and staff. Later the Convener addressed the hourly paid on the sports field, arms flailing and voices raised. We the management team watched this from the cricket pavilion. At four o'clock the Convener reported that the industrial employees would offer no support and would continue to cross the picket lines. The staff's strike would of course now fail, as the vital aspects of the business needed to keep things rolling were being carried out by management and non-union staff. Unionized staff amounted to 66%, but fell after the strike to 30%.

The problem now was to find a solution that allowed the officer to suggest a return to work without changing the final offer in accordance with my mandate, but at the same time producing a face-saving way forward for the officer. Equally difficult was getting the directors of Central, including the Production Director, who no doubt would have one of his demented moments, to agree. I never once considered asking my boss Colin Ions what he thought.

In my early days in Industrial Relations I had been told that a prerequisite of the Personnel Manager's job was to think of solutions when others could not, and this was definitely one of those occasions. The same guy rang an hour after the strike started and said "Make sure you have space to think". Well, not much of that available. Straight from the pavilion to a meeting with the directors, oh and that boss of mine. The industrials had received a 6.6% increase. Hanson had decreed that the maximum for staff would be 6%, though previously staff could always rely on their deal being a rubber-stamp of the industrials' award.

During these negotiations the staff incremental increases had been declared unfair. They were based on service years and were annually increased, which meant that after fifteen years the salary was £1500 more than someone who was totally competent but had only been in the job for a year. Continuation of this automatic £100 increase was being brought to an end. The Trade Union Officer had been infuriated by the company position.

There was no time before meeting the directors to come up with a plan and in any event when I did, I would want to sign if off with the main board Personnel Director before getting the local directors to agree. On the two-hour journey home there was space to think. In the end my solution was a significant stretch of the truth, and I would have to hope no one examined it too closely. The solution came via the shift allowances. These allowances related directly to the type of shift individuals worked and were based on the hourly-paid shift rates, regardless of status or salary, and applied to all three categories of employees, hourly paid, staff and management. There was no formal agreement for staff but the common tie had been adopted since the brewery opened. The suspension of incremental increases could be eased, though not in this year's settlement, but I would give the Trade Union Officer my word that some easing would occur in the 1987 review. The words to be used by the officer to staff were simply that management agreed to review the position of incremental increases at the 87 review. Now for the truth stretch. Shift allowances were paid mainly to brewery quality control staff and primary fleet staff who covered the 24-hour operation, and all worked for the Production Director.

The costings showed that if I froze the staff shift pay at 1986 levels I could increase the staff salaries to 6.3% without overspending on my mandate. The sums were tight and would not stand close examination, but we had a strike no one wanted and I judged no one would closely examine my revamped deal. I got the green light from the Personnel Director of Courage UK and arranged to meet Brian Revell at his office at one o'clock.

I met with the local directors to put my plan forward, and after the Production Director had thrown the baby out of the pram because his staff would suffer and my boss had been supportive, if only via absolute silence, he said he would write down exactly what I said. Fortunately no reply was necessary, as the most senior director present, George Bowsfield, MD for Managed,

Tenanted and Free Trade Central, said "No need for that Colin, I think Mike can handle this don't you?" There was an almost imperceptible nod from Colin, at which point I said I had to be on my way. George said "Good luck Mike, I'll have a drink waiting when you get back". George was a throwback to the early days of my joining Courage, and frequently ended the day full of alcohol and totally relaxed.

On arrival the officer was very hostile. He had been let down by zero support from the industrial employees, and knowing I had little to give and with no relationship having been built between us (after all I had been in Reading for just two months), this was going to be difficult. He immediately produced a recorder. My response was simply "Whatever I say will remain said. I am offended by the slur, unless it is yourself you do not trust". He was white with anger, but the recorder was turned off and placed in his desk. Regardless of how difficult or angry he might be he had nowhere to go. He had no support from within his organization and none from staff, who simply wanted to go back to work. I rolled out the solution quietly, not vindictively, and was marginally apologetic. We had to work together in the future.

The initial hostility intensified upon hearing the way forward. I said "Look Brian, management did not want to offer this solution. I have had to argue for three days simply to find some form of easement so that I would be allowed to present this way forward. The shift pay will be realigned in 1987. The abolition of incremental increases will be slowed, by how much I simply don't know, and hopefully Mr Hanson will have settled down and we can establish some sensible rapport".

Brian snapped "Highly unlikely". I continued talking. "There is little else to offer Brian, and I am sure with your skills you can dress this up to at least look like a sensible interim way forward. I need to hear from you before I leave this office that you accept the deal and that you will press for an immediate return to work. The alternative is no deal and management will address the staff through written communication to say there is no change to the company's offer and failure to return to work may result in the loss of their jobs."

His anger at the latter suggestion, which I had no authority to make, was volcanic. Having let him rant and rave for a while, I suggested we had discussed the matter sufficiently. He was off to Germany to see his daughters on Tuesday evening, so I quietly said "Tuesday morning would be a good time to sort it". He could not go on holiday with staff still on strike. "I will ask the Senior Staff Rep to report back to you after our meeting" he said. "The staff will return to work."

I kept a straight face, though a smile and a raised clenched fist were bursting to get out.

On my return to the brewery I went to my office first rather than meet with the directors. I made everyone in the personnel office aware that I was not present if anyone rang. An hour later I made my way across to the directors, who had been waiting in the MD's office for me to return. I was met in the outer office by my boss. "Deal done" I said. "You had better undo your tie to make it look like it was a tough deal" he said.

Everyone wanted to know every detail of the settlement. George, God bless him, said "Never mind that, I expect Mike could do with a beer and five minutes to gather his thoughts, and then perhaps another beer before we get on with the business". Great fellow George, loved his beverage. His office had its own wine, spirits and beer cabinet.

I told them exactly what I had said to consternation on my boss's face. He had not liked the threat of dismissal. The Production Director did not like the promise of incremental re-introduction. But George loved it all. I stayed to seven drinking with him and then left for home.

Next day I was off on holiday, having only been married for three days and already missed two days of my holiday. It never was of course a honeymoon, but it was our first holiday together as a family.

House hunting was still in full flow, but although the search continued, the problem of the ownership of Forge House remained. For some inexplicable reason Maggie, Lawrence's second wife, had refused to hand over the deeds to either Christine or Michael, her brother, although she had given Lol her deeds just a few days after Lawrence's funeral. Lawrence's will had been in total favour of his second wife and there was no money or provision for the house deeds in the will, which he had made only a few weeks before his death. Our solicitor had recommended we try and resolve the issue alongside Mrs P's settlement, as Lawrence had been paying her a small monthly sum for maintenance. There seemed no appetite for this on the family's part, or for that matter on the part of Mrs P's Barrister.

Peculiarly, I had been rung during the settlement discussions by Mrs P's solicitor acting on the instructions of her barrister. The reason for the call was strange. The solicitor had found it impossible to work with Michael and the barrister had banned him from their meetings. The solicitor had wondered if it was possible for me to talk to Mrs P about the settlement. An offer had been made and the solicitor told me Mrs P appeared to find it acceptable.

I was immediately suspicious about the offer. If Mrs P found it acceptable and her own barrister and solicitor found it acceptable, then why was I being involved in the process? Clearly Michael must have felt it was not right. To ask him would only upset his ego, so it was a presumption I had to run with. The contact must have been made because we shared the same firm of solicitors and perhaps the solicitor did not feel the deal was right.

I asked how much was being offered and indicated that Mrs P's mind would not be on the matter just now as her brother had just died. I listened to the offer, which seemed totally unacceptable. The solicitor was less than forthcoming on his own view of the offer. Lawrence had been a millionaire and shared five children with her, and the house she lived in was in trust to her children. I said I could not recommend this to Mrs P, moreover I would actively discourage a settlement at this level given Mrs P's life expectancy and Lawrence's wealth.

The solicitor then asked what I thought was acceptable and I said that the settlement was for a lifetime, Lawrence had been incredibly wealthy and they shared five children. It should at least be double and if the barrister had a good day triple. The solicitor agreed that that sounded reasonable. I can only assume from his response that he had indeed felt the so-called acceptable offer was not.

Mrs P settled at the doors of the court. I don't know how much the final settlement was, I never asked. All I ever said to Mrs P was "Go to court, I am sure they will settle before you go in".

Now I have wandered from the script a little but Forge House was still an issue. Maggie had been to court a year before and won an uncontested victory (our solicitor forgot to turn up). On this basis our solicitor had the decision put aside. My solicitor felt the case of ownership with no mortgage was very solid, but still Maggie would not give up the deeds. The problem was finally settled by the introduction of a trust for Kirstie, Scott and James.

Even then Maggie tried to be excessively difficult. It was agreed that upon the sale of Forge House I would deposit the sum of £9700, the price of the house originally, into a trust fund to be shared by my children when they reached 21. Then I received a phone call from my solicitor to say that agreement had broken down and Mrs Potter's solicitors were instructed to ask for a deposit of £19,400, double the original price.

"Now Mr Fergie" I said. "I am entirely fed up with this woman and her behaviour. You are therefore instructed to inform her solicitor that in the absence of an immediate agreement at £9700 I will take this story to the *Bristol Evening Post*, where I have an influential friend who is a reporter. Not to put too fine a point on it, I will ensure everyone locally becomes aware of this through the press (actually it was our Courage Press Officer, Bruce Lewis, who had the contact, but he was a good mate). Mr Fergie replied that he understood, and the following day the original agreement was confirmed. Incidentally Mike Potter's settlement was identical. Sadly the Trusts for the children never gained the interest I had hoped for, but each was glad of the cash.

The house-hunting was proving difficult. The rules of the company stated that you had to live within a 25-mile radius of your workplace to qualify for HPA (house purchase allowance). The HPA was a generous package and included a five-year differential payment, thus allowing you to move to a more costly area without loss of income, plus £5000 moving expenses. The houses however were proving too costly, on average being more than double, sometimes treble, the value of Forge House and certainly no larger. In the end we bought a house on the outskirts of Calne in a place called Quemerford, an ugly house, according to the company surveyor employed to establish the HPA differential, in an area where houses were lower in value, but with half an acre it provided a great garden. Twenty years later that garden gave up a little more than the HPA differential that would have been available had we moved say to Newbury, Reading or Lambourne - more about that later. Time to return to Berkshire and the new job.

I was to spend the best part of six years in this role and I have to say it was like working with an open sore. Part of the job was to introduce a Pay and Productivity deal across the entire Bargaining Unit. A Bargaining Unit was a collection of Operational Sites which had a common set of pay rates and conditions which were reviewed annually via negotiations with the appropriate Trade Unions. The leading union was the T & G, the second largest the Amalgamated Engineering Union (AEU). In the Central Bargaining Unit, Beckett was the Convener and Revell the lead T & G Officer. I was not able to build a working relationship with either, the only time throughout my 22 years with the company that this happened. The sites were very diverse in activity and therefore had in many instances separate Operating Agreements which dictated things like length of working day, holiday arrangements, temporary labour and the way in which actual work was issued and undertaken. The sites were quite variable in operation and included a Shire Horse Centre, Distribution Depots, Building Department, Brewing, Primary Fleet and Technical Services, the latter being the guys who installed and maintained beer dispensing equipment in pubs.

Having successfully negotiated the Industrial Employees' annual review in 1987 and cleaned up the staff problems of 86 in their review of 87, I turned my attention to the Pay and Productivity project, which I had been appointed to deliver. In truth this was a much bigger task than I had realized. David Oakley my number two, though a great fellow, had no experience of this type of scheme, nor did young Williams straight out of university, and my boss stood a mile off the project, which was named Mansell,. The name was chosen by the Production Director, who was an avid fan of Grand Prix racing and of Nigel Mansell, one of the great English Formula One drivers of the time.

There was absolutely no appetite for Mansell among the site/functional directors and the senior management had to be driven constantly with little commitment. The exercise was based on work measurement, which lent itself to Technical Services, Distribution and Warehousing, but was much more problematical when applied to production, which was driven by process time namely the output time of machinery, actual processing time, brewing and eventually the men's input/output.

The influence of the men on the overall output still had a significant impact on productivity. The shop Stewards were keenly interested throughout and the production Stewards were very keen to learn about the application of work measurement (the standards applied to their work). This interest was not an acceptance of the Pay and Productivity scheme –in fact the more knowledge they had the better equipped they would be to argue against the final findings. Those findings ultimately would suggest a reduction of 122, men the majority coming from brewing and the closure of Luggershall Depot, which would yield 36 of the total. Project Mansell was signed off by the Courage Board of directors in the late summer of 87, but was never to be implemented.

Before we could go to the Trade Unions my mentor, the Courage Personnel Director, was forced to resign following his refusal as a Trustee of the Courage Pension Fund to allow Hanson plc to raid the fund to the tune of £60million. His position on the Board becoming untenable. He was an honorable man, rare in the business I worked in or indeed any business. It is nearly always self first, then company and finally the employees. This left me even more exposed at Berkshire, as I had always been able to give him a call and release some of the pressure on myself.

Back to Project Mansell. I recall we met the Trade Union representatives in a hotel just outside Reading, first having an evening meal and then giving them an overview of the project. The Trade Unions were not given precise numbers, though Beckett, the Convener, was aware of them. We informed the TU of the intended closure of Luggershall and the forward programme for implementation. The pre-info process for Trade Union Officials was a time-honored tradition and we left them to discuss what we had said. Returning just after eleven, the bastards had walked out on David and me, something I have never experienced before or since. At eleven thirty that evening I rang the new Personnel Director to inform him of the events and he simply said "Get a good night's sleep, we will speak in the morning".

At 3 am David Oakley burst into my bedroom and said "I've had a thought, Mike."

"Forget it David, I'm straight" I said. I got up, got dressed, ordered coffee from the night porter and we went over and over the events of the evening.

Did I make a mistake in not giving them a precise breakdown of the job losses? Did I make a mistake in having a meal first? Yes. Was I as prepared and as professional as I could have been? No. There would be no recovery from this setback, it cost me a promotion to Area Personnel Manager Central, and clearly the new Personnel Director for Courage, who had written the infamous Blue Book that dictated terms and conditions in Central, was not comfortable with my management of the project. Moreover he was a massive mate of Beckett, the Convener, who by now barely spoke to me.

Project Mansell had unearthed many corrupt practices, particularly within Berkshire Brewery. This was Europe's premier brewery, but with some industrial employee earnings hitting £40,000 pa (remember this was 1988) it was not commercially viable. It closed in 2010, a victim of its impossible pay structure and Trade Union blindness (no not really). The S&N Board of directors had attempted to show the City and the brewing industry that they could take very big decisions. Heineken, the new owners of S&N, stated after the takeover that it would not have been a decision they would have taken, and there was no fundamental commercial reason for this action. Project Mansell would not have cured all the ills of Berkshire Brewery, but it might have paved the way for a much more productive unit.

The new Personnel Director had, under the influence of the Convener (I am sure), suggested to me that I could not negotiate, and my approach was to take no prisoners. I angrily reeled off my successes and challenged him to name anyone who had equalled the list. He was taken aback. He was of course a bully and found my directness difficult to cope with.

I was to have four bosses before Project Mansell was put to bed, very different from the paper I had originally presented to the Courage Board. The strains of Mansell saw Beckett fall by the wayside. The newly elected Convener, Alan Jones, a man with principles akin to my own (thank god), was much easier to work with. Along the way there were to be a few successes, including the introduction of a performance-based appraisal scheme for staff, the first in the company, the introduction of qualified training instructors from the industrial workforce for the industrial workforce, another first and genuine recognition from local directors for my contribution to annual pay reviews. The Production Director became ever more hostile and made life more and more difficult, but my time was coming in respect of this individual following an extraordinary event on the production line.

My wife was busy bringing up the family and having to cope with my frustration at work when I returned home often after nine in the evening. I had little energy at home, but I did make and install a kitchen and build a fireplace in the lounge. During my time at Berkshire I seriously sought employment with other companies on three occasions, reaching the final interview stage twice with other brewers, but with no success, which did not help my morale.

Reflecting on the Personnel Director's comments, it was true that I felt diplomacy was for those who did not believe in their own opinions, and when it came to my diplomacy it was often delivered in a "machete manner" without care what its impact might be. In the years at Berkshire I had become irritable, intolerant and overly confident of my own opinion. The result was that I made many enemies among the senior management and even directors - unhealthy, you bet it was. Strangely no such issues existed with the lower ranks of management or for that matter with any of the shop Stewards (with whom I had built exceptionally good working relationships), so much so that they trusted me to correct the misdemeanours of other employees when line management failed to do so. When employees abused the sickness scheme unfairly as viewed by their shop Steward, or put the scheme in jeopardy in some way, the Stewards would tell me and ask me to intervene. These requests were secretive and management often wondered how I could be so well informed. Such an incident was to lead to the demise of the demented Production Director.

Chris Cole, the Personnel Services Manager, who had been at the brewery since it opened and a further thirty years before that at Bridge Street Brewery in Reading town centre, came to me on the first day of my boss's holiday (he was to be away for three weeks) with a story - and what a story it was. One of the operatives from the bottling hall had come to see him to tell him (he had known Chris for twenty years) that another bottling operative was urinating on the line, and he was unsure what to do about it. This of course would have been a public relations disaster for the company had it got into the media. Where was line management on this one? They all knew, but the Production Director had forbidden any of them from telling me. Equally important, they were doing nothing about the problem, which according to the informant was continuing unabated.

When Chris told me I knew the Production Director was in trouble, though I did not know about his edict to keep it secret at this stage. This guy had given me a lot of grief and nothing I did now was about to help him. I saw the informant with Chris away from site. The man was genuinely terrified of being identified. The perpetrator was a nasty piece of work, and equally the informant did not want to be seen to be someone who grassed on his mates. I was to refer to this informant throughout the whole saga as witness J. I promised him his name would not be divulged to anyone unless we had to go to an Industrial Tribunal, which was of course held in the public domain, and if sufficiently juicy (and it certainly would be), a full press report would follow and this one would go national.

The Shop Steward for the packaging section said he had not seen anything as he worked on opposite shifts to the offender and did not want to be involved. I was not able to ascertain why he wanted to be kept out of any investigative/Shop Steward role relating to this case, but he was adamant that he wanted no involvement. I gathered further statements quietly and semi secretively from other witnesses, who were each given a letter to hide their identity, though many statements were of no use. After conducting many interviews, there was only one other witness (witness W) whose evidence confirmed the gross act, and he was more frightened of being called a grass by his mates than our original witness J. I was not sure I could get him to sign a statement, in which case his evidence would not be admissible at an Industrial Tribunal.

When I approached the senior manager for packaging, he told me the Production Director had said no one was to speak about the incident and in particularly not to me, and if they did and he found out he would make sure they lost their job. I smiled. At eleven o'clock that evening I rang the Production Director at his home and suggested he made sure that he contact his boss to make him aware of the incident on the bottling line, as I would be taking the necessary actions to bring the matter under control in the morning. The Production Director said, and I quote him verbatim nearly twenty years later, "I manage Berkshire Brewery, not you, and don't ever fucking ring me again at home". I knew he was making a very big mistake but I thought of him as no more than an absolute wanker and, please excuse the pun, thought he deserved no more than to be tossed overboard.

One minute after this conversation I spoke to the Personnel Director, Graham Kendrick, at home and relayed the problem. His reaction was, "Mike we will have to be extremely careful, this has the makings of a public relations disaster. I will speak with you again in the morning but with your boss away safe delivery of this situation will be on your shoulders". Great pressure, but I felt in control.

At 9.30 Graham rang. He said I have spoken to Peter Ward (the Production Director's boss), who knew nothing whatsoever about this. "The Production Director is finished Mike but we must keep him on board until this matter is safely concluded" he said. "The Production Director will this morning be told by Peter Ward that in regards of this matter he must act in accordance with your wishes and instructions at all times. I want you to ring me at 11.30 with your plan to bring this to a swift conclusion. Our PR Manager is preparing statements for the press should the issue blow up. Don't let it blow up Mike."

I rang Graham at 11.29 and told him my intention was to call a disciplinary hearing at 3 pm. There would be no suspension, as it would only allow the offender to talk to all and sundry. I said I was going to select a shop Steward who had sufficient balls to see this through to a conclusion, and that conclusion would be a resignation by the offender today.

Graham interrupted me, saying "You be absolutely sure the shop Steward scares the living daylights out of him Mike. Threaten to take him through the courts if he ever utters a word. Threaten to ruin his life if he ever speaks publicly to anyone about this issue. You understand what I am saying Mike?"

He asked me if I thought I could really force a resignation and my reply was that the shop Steward once in possession of the facts would do that.

At 2.05 the shop Steward I had selected to handle the problem walked into my office and I explained the situation.

"I hope you are going to help me save the reputation of this brewery and this company" I said. I told him about the plan for a mock Stage 4 disciplinary at which the person to be dismissed would not be allowed to be present, though he would be in the office next door. He would be brought across by his manager at 4 o'clock, and the manager would stay with him until Terry was ready to see him. Terry looked at me and asked if I've stayed in the sample room too long (suggesting I had sampled too much beer). Terry was an upright fellow with a keen interest in birds, so we shared a common hobby, and he had been one of the first to volunteer to be an Operations Training Instructor. He had balls, so he was just the fellow for this outing.

I relayed the problems on the bottling and canning lines (we doubted if any urine had ever entered the cans or bottles of beer despatched for sale to the public). The individual had been seen using drains, and on at least one occasion an empty can. Disbelief and horror rolled across Terry's face. I read the two significant statements, informing Terry one was signed and the other required signature. All statements were prefixed with an identification letter. I did of course have statements with actual names and a signature, a fact I was to deny later.

"Jesus, I've got to take a hell of a lot on trust Mike" he said.

"Not really Terry, I would never have called you to this office and told you this story if every bit of it was not true."

I explained that during the mock stage 4 the Personnel Services Manager would be there taking notes, along with the Packaging Manager and us two. There would be no other conversation with anyone while it was going on

"You may ask as many questions as you wish Terry, but don't make them difficult" I said. "Remember you are going to get the individual to admit to this gross act and then persuade him to resign. I know it's a tough ask but I also know you can do it. The Stage 4 hearing is a complete charade. It will however allow the line management, yourself and personnel to hear the case and produce a record should this go tits up. I asked for your help because I know you have the intellect and the balls to carry it through." Terry smiled.

At 3 o'clock the hearing started. I read every single statement slowly and deliberately, and the Senior Manager from Packaging was very surprised at the weight of evidence. I turned to Terry and told him that the individual accused of these heinous acts was sitting next door, the evidence against him was irrefutable. I said I had no wish to reconvene this hearing and I expected the man to resign.

One hour later Terry reported back that the offender had admitted to the indecent act and would remain totally silent about his behaviour. Terry asked if we could we supply a reference, and I responded that we would supply one appropriate to the requesting companies' needs but that we would not support by a reference any application for a job that involved the individual working within a factory producing food, drink or food-related products. I did not indicate what the reference would say. The commitment was disingenuous but this issue had to be screwed down very tightly and a silly argument over a reference might unhinge the whole process. I thanked Terry for his help and asked that he leave the events of the last three hours locked up in his head. I also asked him to get the man to write out and date his resignation. No one on the site ever spoke again about the incident.

The Senior Packaging Manager enquired as to whether or not the events that had just taken place constituted a disciplinary hearing. I replied that a full stage 4 hearing had been obviated by the resignation of the offender. What a knob the SPM was!

Graham Kendrick was pleased about the result but it made little difference to his overall opinion of me, probably reaffirmed when I refused point blank to give up the names of the employees who had witnessed the misdemeanour.

The company launched a full investigation into the events, headed by the Group Security Officer and the Group Employee Relations Manager. In hindsight the enquiry was partly required to discover more about the Production Director's cover up, and of course to learn lessons about how we might handle such an event better in the future. I could not see how the enquiry would benefit from me giving up the names of the informants.

I had given my word and my intention was to keep it. I informed the Group Employee Relations Manager accordingly and confirmed to him that I had destroyed the original file containing all names and contacts. I subsequently posted the Working File, which contained identical information, with all industrial employees known only by their identifying letter. Tom, the Group Employee Relations Manager, later informed me that my actions had pissed off Mr Kendrick, and my response was "So be it Tom". I had given my word, and at Berkshire Brewery the incident was never again a point of conversation.

Working Life at Berkshire might have been difficult at times but it was never dull. David Oakley, now promoted to Area Distribution Manager Central, informed me that some form of empties scam was taking place at the Brooklands Depot. Having not long sorted the 'pee in a can' fiasco, now we had disappearing empty beer bottles - not a few but 40-foot long trunker loads, literarily thousands upon thousands. Oakley as usual was sure of his facts but had no facts, only hearsay. The Brooklands Depot was notorious for stock losses and David wondered if I could have a look at the problem. I am of course a personnel manager (as David Oakley was previously, having been my number two) not a distribution expert, and barely understood the information on a delivery note, let alone stock discrepancy errors therein, but common sense told me that the delivery note was key as it recorded fulls out and empties returned. Empty bottles had a value, as they were reused many times.

Oakley, in his attempt to establish the truth, had draymen from Reading Depot secretly loading vehicles with fictitious returns, which demonstrated that some of the recorded deliveries simply would not have fitted on to the vehicle. 'Oakers' instructs the great sleuth Vic Bassey, Group Security Officer, to follow and spy on the Brooklands draymen and interview the Depot Manager about returns. He in turn briefed all the employees about the need for accurate returns and the fact that there was a major stock loss, though this briefing had been done on five previous occasions. Oakley had also been told by an ex-Brooklands driver, now retired, that a transport manager, previously a shop Steward at the depot, was involved in the scam. The investigation included the interviewing of every single drayman, but three weeks of observation by "Vic the sleuth" brought forward no evidence against any individual.

Oakley meanwhile was revving up his engines in order to resolve the problem and steamed into my office to update me. "Well Boydie, what are we going to do about it?" he asked me. I pointed out that the problem had been around for nearly 10 years, accountants, security and previous distribution management having failed to get to grips with it. I suspected, but did not know, that the answer lay in the delivery note detail. We knew that the number of alleged returns on some occasions would not have fitted on to the vehicles. We knew the problem had been happening on and off for 10 years. We knew the stock losses for bottles were astronomical. A retired draymen had given us some names of offenders, but no clues as to how the discrepancies were occurring.

I suggested we should have two dedicated distribution experts, an office and five months of delivery notes checked, and I meant every single delivery note. I wanted a table of fulls delivered and a table of empties recorded as returned from each pub, as extracted from each delivery note. Then I wanted the differences logged against every drayman. While they were at it, I wanted the pubs with the largest discrepancies identified. Oakley asked how long it would take, and I said "Not as long as the bloody fiddle has been going on for".

Six weeks later we had our league tables and three crews (draymen operate in pairs) and two pubs stood out like sore thumbs, with massive ins and outs discrepancies. The investigation provided the potential for six industrial dismissals, one transport manager, one managed house manager (pub manager employed by the company) and the prosecution of a tenanted pub manager for fraud, with the possibility against that that the company could be liable for £360,000 in compensation if the case went in favour of the dismissed employees at an Industrial Tribunal. This would need signing off at Courage MD level. The cost did not include the legal and court fees involved with removing and prosecuting the tenant, who was not of course an employee.

In order to take this forward in a way that was manageable for me and at the same time under my total control, I had to fix the thought process of the Courage Operations Director and my old Mate Graham Kendrick, the Courage Personnel Director. My boss in fairness was supportive of my actions throughout. To achieve the fix, I simply wrote to Oakley copying the Ops Director, Personnel Director and my boss labeling the memo 'secret' and setting down in print the precise course of action necessary to allow an industrial tribunal to observe through the memo (no emails at this time) that the company had followed a thorough, unbiased and technically correct approach throughout the proceedings. This approach also ensured, through a specific reference to the tenant, that we had sought to take action but had been advised by the police that insufficient criminal evidence existed.

An employer has only to demonstrate that it is "reasonable to believe" an employee has committed an offence, not prove it as required in a civil or criminal law case. With this case it was very much based on reasonable belief. My memo, which was rewritten four times before publication and delivery, was accepted as the way forward. The Ops Director, Chris Pavlosky requested a meeting with myself and Oakers before nodding through the approach.

I had met Chris for the first time in the Courage

boardroom at Staines, about three months after his appointment from Dixons. 'Pavo', as he was affectionately known, had upon joining the company launched a work study examination of all central warehouse operations via an outside consultancy. We had our own in-house work study team and all distribution delivery work was work studied. The warehouse operations did not apply the study results to operational pay or hours of work, but it was a significant tool in establishing manpower. No doubt the Ops Director felt a quick win could be achieved, particularly in warehousing via manpower requirements.

The guy presenting the findings for the consultancy was the most pompous and condescending person I had met in a long time, and the bastard had been dismissive of my comments at the commencement of the exercise. I knew because of all the work measurement exposure I had experienced in Courage West that the report contained major blunders, and so did our in-house study guys. He was moving towards his summary, namely how many men could be taken out of the operation, when one of our in-house work study managers suggested we should check the report with regard to some of the conclusions.

Pavo asked with a certain testiness why this was necessary, saying he had read the report from front to back at least three times. I told him to look at page 12, last two paragraphs, page 13 first two paragraphs, the last sentence in each of the paragraphs. Pavo responded

"Now that's sharp really sharp". The consultant looked mortified. There were huge errors in this element of the report, in fact so calamitous that the facts might well have been dragged from another exercise. The consultant accused the management team of setting an elephant trap, but he was no longer pompous and condescending, having seen his report destroyed in a few sentences and his usefulness to Pavo zeroed. I am not sure he had even read the report before presenting its findings.

Pavo asked the consultant to step into one of the meeting rooms adjacent to main boardroom. On his return he sat quietly for a moment before summarising. I stood up to leave the boardroom to go the toilet, having motioned my apologies to Pavo, but as I opened the door the darkness appeared odd. Then I was suddenly showered with broom handles - I had walked into the bloody cleaner's cupboard and all its contents now spewed into the boardroom. From pin-sharp to stupid in less than five minutes. No one laughed, but everyone's face told a story. Oakers came to my rescue, ushering me out of the correct door. Pavo decided that the manpower figures could not be used at this time and said he would revisit the problem very shortly.

Back now to the empties scam. Two months after I had written the memo and Oakers had first brought the problem to me, we suspended the six draymen, who on average had each returned some 1750 more cases of empty bottles over the five-month period than they had delivered. I simply drew a line under these six. The average surplus for all the other draymen was 63, so the difference was glaringly obvious. You had to suspect that everyone had dabbled in it some time in the year, but it was difficult to sustain reasonable belief among our investigating team (let alone an IT Panel) that a variance of 63 constituted fraud on the part of every drayman, as it was less than one case every other trip. Discrepancies at this level could be assigned to poor counting or just occasionally being paired with a rogue drayman. All cases of bottles of course carried a monetary value which was credited to the pub, and draymen were given a share of this credit.

All the six suspended draymen were ultimately dismissed. The Transport Manager resigned (he admitted to receiving £45 a month) and the managed house manager's contract was rescinded (he had not been permanent but had been at the pub for three years). The tenant got away with it. The stock-losses ceased without further reappearance, and one of the investigating managers became the new depot manager.

All the draymen appealed to an Industrial Tribunal for unfair dismissal. We hired a very expensive solicitor who in turn hired a very expensive barrister named Chris Jeans, who had worked on many of the Wapping print industry dismissals. We produced a 500-page bundle of evidence) for the Tribunal and tried to get the cases joined (all heard together), but one drayman refused, the brother of Oakley's original informant. We all travelled to London on the Sunday evening for the case, scheduled for a five day hearing (we being Chris Cole, dismissing manager, Mick Ellmer and Peter Isaac, investigating managers, Oakers and myself), staying at the Holiday Inn. We had an evening meal which was appalling. When we complained we were given two bottles of wine on the night and when I wrote a letter of complaint, Lorraine and I were offered a free weekend at the hotel. There was unfortunately an American band staying at the hotel and they played until 3 am, so we got very little sleep.

At five thirty Oakers and I strolled up to the Thames and wondered how the day would go. The Industrial Tribunal panel was made up of three people. The legal person who chaired it was a woman who was infamous for her strange decisions and outrageous comments, so much so that she had been mentioned in Private Eye on a number of occasions. The other two would commonly be a retired Personnel Manager and a Trade Unionist typically branch secretary or ex Officer.

At nine o'clock we met with Chris Jeans and Andrew Lilly, the solicitor. We were off to a great start when the barrister spotted an error in our figures - very important, because it was in our delivered/returned table, absolutely key to our case. After some twenty minutes Chris Cole realised it was simply no more than a typing error, so we amended it.

Jeans advised us that we had less than a 5 per cent chance of winning and advised us to settle now, thus avoiding a potentially very heavy compensation package to the dismissed employees. I could see the colour drain from Oakley's face. We had ten minutes, and decided to go for a walk to discuss it.

As we hit the street, I lit my ninth cigarette of the morning, dragged deeply and turned to David. "Before you say a word, we have not come all this way to go home" I said. "We are going to open the batting." I chose those words because David was an excellent cricketer, hitting centuries in three consecutive years during company tournaments. He responded with a smile. "You bet we're going to bat Mike."

Two days later we had won the case. The chair commended the company on its investigation and the barrister earned £75,000 for his troubles.

I celebrated the result a wee bit too much. I was drunk on the way back to Paddington and had to open the cab door wide to be sick with Chris Cole holding onto to me for dear life.

As we rolled into 1992, the job at Berkshire was finally coming together with the demented Production Director having left and likewise Beckett, the man with indefinable principles. The air was clearing. The appointment of an old colleague from the West as the new Production Director was a real help. Jim Gardener had previously been Production Director at Bath Street, Bristol, and we had had a very good working relationship. I recall one Christmas turning up for an afternoon meeting with him wearing a pair of frog earrings left over from the Personnel lunch. Jim never said a word until I was leaving his office, upon which he suggested I drop my mates off at a local pond.

However things were always changing. We were merging with Grand Met (producers of Watney Red Barrel) and my boss, who I got on with pretty well, rang me while I was on holiday and said I had to attend a meeting tomorrow to be interviewed by a Personnel panel for a new position following agreement on a new personnel structure. There was to be a 40% cull of personnel jobs following the merger. Personnel were going first so they could lead the merger of the company's other sectors, starting with Sales.

My presentation in truth was poor, and as I had had no inkling of this structure change, my guess was that I was an outsider for any of the new positions. Berkshire had harmed my reputation, and this might well be curtains. My boss seemed keen for me to take on a London job, where for the most part the industrial relations scene was the pits. However when pushed on this, I simply said that accommodation of an acceptable standard would be beyond my means and that I had no desire to live in or near the city of London. Job gone, I thought, but the position of Employee Relations Manager West and Wales was offered and accepted. Six years after leaving for Reading I was back in the West, and with the same boss I had had previously and basically the same job, though this time the status was at senior management level and the area covered now encompassed the Midlands, Reading and the South Coast as well as the West and South Wales. The move was clearly sideways, but it kept the mortgage payments going and I was back among many of my old working colleagues.

Berkshire had been a grim experience for most of the time, and while I had had some successes, I had also been overlooked for promotion on a number of occasions. The reason for being overlooked was almost certainly my volatile attitude and less than diplomatic dismissal of some directors' and their opinions or even instructions. This was no way to climb the ladder, even if you have a smidgin of talent.

Berkshire though was not all dark days. I had learned to write my own material and how to influence the course of events without the consent of my superiors, and this in itself felt good.

Just occasionally at Berkshire a fun event would come along and I recall one such event with a real smile. It occurred on an open day for the workforce and their families. One of the day's events was the driving of an articulated lorry, much favoured by the ladies in attendance and carried out under the expert tutelage of our resident driving instructor. All good intentions were blown out of the water when one of the ladies found the co-ordination of steering and throttle a little confusing. An almighty bang resounded round the site as she hit the warehouse wall and continued to demolish the outer wall for some fifty feet before Reg the driving instructor, regained control.

As the vehicle demolished the wall and it fell away, hundreds upon hundreds of empty beer cans spilled across the road. Their contents were drunk by the operatives and the cans deposited into the cavity wall that rose just six feet on the inside.

On another occasion a paintball day was arranged for a Saturday in late February as a team-building exercise. Attendance was not mandatory, but the duty managers were the only ones not present, despite the very cold weather. The event was run for brewing management with all personnel management invited. It is amazing how quickly the adrenalin surges through you. Most of us behaved as if we were super-fit marines and with an endless supply of paint-balls (all were free) our enthusiasm knew no bounds. I remember the Head Brewer hurtling through the woods like Arnold Schwarzenegger, destroying undergrowth, breaking branches and yelling like the wild man of Borneo. I turned, rolled on my back and shot him all in one motion, hitting him under the right armpit, in the chest and between the legs. He yelled in pain and looked at me in total disbelief. The adjudicator declared him dead. Walking back through the woods I could hear him shouting, "Mike Boyd shot me, Mike Boyd is in personnel, Mike Boyd is on my side!"

On the day we won six of the seven games with the opposition refusing to come out of their camp on the seventh game. For a week after the event it was virtually the only topic that everyone talked about. My boss had to take the lift to the office for several days, as he was so stiff he was unable to cope with the stairs. Sadly the team spirit built that day could not withstand the pressures of everyday operational management.

Back home, Lorraine seemed to be in absolute control and of course I was getting used to my extended family, although at this time we saw very little of them. Bill was still in the army and Brian and Joanne were in Ramsgate, as were Lorraine's parents. Her dad was a quiet man, but I instantly got on with my mother-in-law, who was a little more outgoing.

The children were growing up, particularly Kirstie, and I had started to do a bit of fishing with Scott, leaving home at just after 4.30 in the morning to get a good spot on the bank of the Bristol Avon in Wiltshire. We discovered later we were fishing in the wrong place and had been for several years. We were both fined £15 each for having the wrong licence. Most of the fishing was done at Sutton Benger. Fishing did not suit James, although he did try a couple of times. I know I never really spent enough time with my children when they were young and you can never turn the clock back. Nearly all my entire energy was directed towards work.

Before leaving Berkshire Brewery, I was asked to investigate a racist accusation at Tottenham which had allegedly occurred in one of our tenanted pubs, quite why they asked me I don't know. What I did know was that Harringay Racial Equality Council were real sticklers when it came to racism and provided total support to anyone whom they thought had been racially abused. The individual was an Iranian, a District Surveyor, and he had alleged that the ASM (area sales manager), along with the tenant, had left a sum of cash in excess of £50 in a place where the Surveyor would see it, take it and thereby be dismissed for theft, and the reason for doing this was because he was coloured.

This case was rather bizarre, made even more so by a phone call from the West Midlands Police who told me they had received a bomb threat against Tottenham Depot, the base from which the Surveyor worked. Despite some close questioning of the police officer, I could not establish the reality of this threat, so I absurdly decided I would ignore it without ever making any future reference. Some racial accusations are of the oddest nature and are often driven by other issues. The difficulty as I interviewed this particular individual was that a feeling in my own mind persisted – namely, in your own country any complaint and you would probably be locked up, here in England your treatment will be exempt. The facts were that his previous appraisals gave no hint of racism, Tottenham was already multi racial, no one noticed anyone, the ASM was typically a posh version of a car salesman and the Surveyor was insecure. A finely-crafted set of letters and much time spent with the Surveyor kept Harringay REC away. The matter was put quietly to bed and no bomb materialised, thank heavens.

My job now (1992) was to manage industrial peace,

or as the dictionary describes it, to ensure freedom from disturbance. The Trade Unions were still highly active and the management maintained total reverence with regard to their importance and power. This despite Mrs Thatcher's efforts to curtail their excesses such as closed shops (no union card, no job) picketing and legislation on strike action. The balance of power was now in reality with management, but my company were still to come to terms with this at the higher echelons of personnel management. Their history was steeped in trouble and strife, and naturally their reference points were of a different era. This continued to influence the company decision-making on the industrial front for many years to come.

To help the reader a little, I need to explain the difference between Operating Agreements and Substantive Agreements. Substantive Agreements contain such elements as disciplinary procedures, redundancy entitlements, pension rights, notice periods, sickness entitlement and sometimes common grade rates for the jobs undertaken, and will typically apply to many different working groups. Operating Agreements may apply to common groups, say distribution in a geographical area, or sometimes to a single distribution depot or warehousing operation. These agreements contain contracted working hours, bank holiday cover and pay. Many would use working standards (measured time to do the job) and stipulate manning levels and any bonus payments. In the main they were the most important to both company and employee, as they dictated output over pay, a conflict that kept me in a job for a long while. The truth was I embraced conflict with no fear and enjoyed a good argument, or for that matter a bad argument. There were plenty of both in my work arena.

The Operating Agreements were often left in situ for many years while unions and management tweaked the edges, frequently to no effect other than to satisfy a work ethic within personnel and/or the boardroom who liked to see matters moving on. They moved on often to nowhere, in particular they led to the mere appearance of activity but with little real progress. For instance in 1979 Reading Depot opened and with it came a new Operating Agreement known as the Distribution Payment System, commonly referred to as the DPS , which was introduced and applied across the Courage Central zone. Brooklands, Luggershall, Chandlers Ford, Brierley Hill, Coventry and Wednesbury operated with this agreement for nearly twenty years, many up to the day they closed. This inertia among the hierarchy of brewing management was replicated in verbatim fashion by most of British management, and industry "contracting out" became the epitome of advancement for many.

In the case of Reading Depot, the tweaking from 1979 onwards was so corrupt that by 1990 the delivery operation had become almost unmanageable, with the employees, various fleet Stewards and the convener attaching restrictive practices to all aspects of the working arrangements, which then became custom and practice agreements, overlaid with yet more disruptive restrictions. All across the company such unattended modernisation of Operating Agreements and unacceptable operating corruptions occurred.

When Scottish and Newcastle bought Courage in 1995, their own Operating Agreement for distribution depots had been in situ since early 1980 and was riddled with restraint, hybridization (post mergers) and unbelievable easements of the original intention, though one must say, there was total denial on the part of Scottish management as to how lax they were, for instance sick pay was payable for up to 52 weeks and the reality was that Scottish management took no action against any employee until they had been absent for 53 weeks - quite incredible. However their takeover was a few years off yet and I had plenty to keep me busy in the new job over the next couple of years.

My return to the West also saw the company endeavouring to give line management a more active role in industrial relations, and for a brief period line management, ie Depot Managers and Technical Service Managers, were given the opportunity to take the lead role in negotiations and in some cases write and introduce new Operating Agreements. I recall riding shotgun on one such set of the negotiations at the Avonmouth depot. The facts were simple - I did not like, nor could I get on with, the Depot Manager, moreover the Operating Agreement he was attempting to negotiate was a carbon copy of the failed London Distribution Agreement (LDA)negotiated in the late eighties.

This was an uncomfortable exercise for me. I could not comprehend the retrograde thought process of a 1980s Operating Agreement being introduced. It was apparent from the start that the Stewards had already identified an earnings cap, as the deal was based on annualised hours and the Trade Union Officer was so well versed in the agreement he could have written it. The reality was that the negotiations were over before they started. Avonmouth employees were accustomed to earning high money and the real grafters very high money; nothing like that was available here. Any close examination of this Agreement would have spelt out disaster to most informed distribution management. Frequently the work was not being completed within the yearly hours available, and as there was no overtime available, time off was being used as a substitute. In London the additional leave became so high it had to be bought out at very high rates year after year. I had many years earlier come across a similar arrangement in the Bath Street Brewery, where overtime worked had been traded for additional holidays, sometimes resulting in an extra month's holiday being credited. It too had to be bought out to maintain sufficient labour availability.

The T & G Officer had communicated in full with the London Transport Convener and knew all the wrinkles, pitfalls, disadvantages and advantages which did not look great to him. The Agreement meant high manning levels, high output levels and modest income compared to what previously had been achieved by the men at Avonmouth. The deal looked like a backward step for the employees and the company. When the Depot Manager posted his best deal, which was traditionally accompanied with the words final offer, the T & G Officer forgot the normal etiquette of retiring to consider the offer before rejecting it. This prompted one of my few interventions, as I suggested that the officer had not fully understood the seriousness of the offer and it might well be worth while consulting the shop Stewards and debating all the alternatives prior to committing to a final response. The Officer responded with the following words, which I recall to this day: "You advise well". The depot manager noted my professional approach, whereby the Trade Union team took a lengthy adjournment before again rejecting the final offer. The manager knew it was curtains for the London lookalike agreement and the practice of putting the line in the chair had taken a big blow in the West and Wales area. In fact not a single Line Lead Agreement was successively achieved across the company during this brief experimental period.

# CHAPTER FIVE

# Tough talking

In January 1993 Lorraine rang to tell me my mother had been taken seriously ill. I was only five minutes from the hospital and arrived at the same time as the ambulance. She was awfully pale, and as they took her from the ambulance she spotted me and simply said "Hello Mike". They were to be the last words she spoke to me, dying just a few days later on my birthday.

My mother was a loving mother, fiercely proud of her children and a beautiful woman in her younger years. She adored all her grandchildren, but had a real soft spot for my sister Kate's children, who lived just along the road.

You know at the point of losing your mother that you have never done enough to repay the hours she nursed you when you were ill, or redress the things she went without so you could be decently attired for school, or said "Thanks Mum" often enough for the way she strived to ensure you always had something special for your birthday. Mums do simple things like loving you very much, which are so important to a child. I could not express a true sense of thanks in my goodbye speech. I am an emotional person just below the surface and it simply bubbled over. Like all mothers, she wanted to be the best mother and to instinctively do the best for her children. She achieved that in abundance and with buckets of love.

In the midst of writing about my mother, I recall an incident from my childhood. Mother was picking me up from yet another stay at Grand's when Mrs Chapman two doors up from Grand's came round with a plate of cakes for Kate, Jenn and myself. Now my mother was deeply religious but equally superstitious. She announced that Mrs Chapman was a witch, and should we eat the cakes we would all fall ill. Mum told Grand to put the cakes on the fire, and as kids we were horrified at seeing our cakes set alight. As we watched the cakes grew rapidly black, black as coal, blistering on the edges, raisins popping like bullets, and then quite frighteningly, one by one they literally exploded into the room. Both my sisters screamed. Mum turned to Grand and said "I told you she was a bloody witch!"

In her later years many people gained the title 'witch' but these were primarily people she did not like, unlike Mrs Chapman, whom I believe she truly thought was a witch.

At Mum and Dad's 40th wedding anniversary I made a short speech thanking them both for always being there whenever one of us needed them - you could ask for no more. My father passed away five years later. I had never shared the same closeness with him as I had with my mother, but when I needed his help he was there.

My father liked to gamble, and on a couple of occasions he took me to the dog racing at Eastville Stadium (the home of Bristol Rovers, until it became a Tesco superstore). I was about eleven on the first occasion and recall being give two shillings (10p) to bet on the dogs and being bought a bag of coconut mushrooms. Amazing what you keep in your memory bank. My most shocking memory though was of seeing Dad seconds after he had passed away. It is a picture that still shocks me. Every ounce of life had drained away, I always wish I had not seen him that way.

Mum and Dad are buried together at East Harptree cemetery. My sister Kate tells me that flowers never stay on the grave and suggests they must be arguing again. Argue they did, but until separated by death they had been married for well over forty years.

I ponder now what Mum and Dad might have thought of their grandchildren, Kirstie, Scott and James. With all three going off to university, there is little doubt that their pride would have been immense. My mother was a very proud woman and I can hear her now telling the neighbours of her grandchildren's achievements. Pictures of them in their graduation gowns would have adorned her walls.

At the beginning of my working life, I had no burning ambitions. Luck, fate and some hard graft got me a half decent career, and with Kirstie, Scott and James, I never pushed them. They all seemed bright enough and university seemed totally natural when it happened. Lorraine and I instilled the fundamentals of right and wrong, and we attended every school review and took full interest in their reports. Most were good as their education evolved, and success was driven from their own desire. Of course today I am immensely proud of my children and my mother would have to take second place in the pride stakes.

As the years roll by you recognise in your children and grandchildren some of your own traits, habits and behaviour and are often shocked by the similarities and amused and secretly pleased by some of the recognitions. As your children grow older they of course make their own decisions. When I advise, sometimes they listen, mostly not. When Kirstie was getting married she had to be in total charge, and there are times when I am much the same, but so was her mother. Evie, my granddaughter, has clearly inherited the 'I'm in charge' attitude. Scott has followed my enjoyment of DIY and house renovation and now advises me, his approach to the work being eerily similar to mine. I note also on occasion that James in debate is as dismissive of the opposing theory, view or opinion as I might once have been, perhaps with less acidity, and there is a canny admission on his part that the Boyd impatience has occasionally to be taken under control when in discussion. All three of my children share my confidence in their own opinion.

★ ★ ★ ★ ★

As I return to my work it is perhaps worth explaining the essence of my job at this juncture, which was to avoid at all times any form of strike action, to facilitate and negotiate annual pay increases for industrial employees and unionised staff, resolve disputes, advise on the correctness or otherwise of dismissals, employment legislation and race relations within the workplace. I also wrote and implemented new agreements, as determined by the company's directions or my own desire to achieve quality change. The MD of West and Wales was Mr customer service personified, and in truth the company was convinced that high quality service would boost sales by retaining and winning new customers. The only issue was how to deliver such service at no additional cost. This was a real opportunity and allowed me a chance to be creative in the preparation of new operating methods and practices that accommodated the customer service drive. For the first time the operation would embrace weekend and evening working, Bank Holiday working and improved service at the call, alongside normal everyday operations, with the same number of men at the same cost as current - improbable but possible. In real terms the cost of the cover could virtually be offset by a single redundancy, retirement, ill health retirement or any other form of manpower reduction.

Technical Services are first to go forward on the highly visible customer service package. I'll have to be careful - there are three totally separate bargaining groups and copycat agreements do lead to an auction house of the best pay and conditions from each agreement. The Trade Union representing each group is the T & G and they will talk to one another via the various officers as we progress negotiations. I give myself a self-imposed goal of six weeks per agreement. The task is to get all groups working weekends and evenings up to 9 pm including Bank Holidays.

The first set of negotiations is concluded at Weston Super Mare. The Officer, after three weeks of intense negotiations meeting twice a week, calls me to one side and says they will settle for an extra £2000 pa to cover the evenings and weekends as written into the Agreement. We will unanimously recommend it to the technicians and believe there is a 95% chance of acceptance. My response was that I could not do that Paul. He looked at me with disbelief and said, "Mike, this is a real runner.

"I know, but I have £2300 to spend per person per annum" I said.

"Well, I'll take that" said Paul with further disbelief. Had I spent less, it is almost certain the monetary values available for the other two agreements would have been reduced pro rata, making my task difficult to nearly impossible. I had struck a very close bond with the officer by offering more than he had asked for. Paul would almost certainly report to the employees that he had asked for £2500 and settled for £2300, and in future deals would know that if I gave him an end figure it was an end figure.

The other groupings were not only different in make-up, ie much younger techs, their background was different; few had come into Technical Services from the trades. Moreover the Convener of Central would be more constrained by the Central Bargaining Unit. In the Midlands the merger had brought together five different sets of techs, all wanting to cherry-pick their way back to pre-merger days. The first agreement was delivered and implemented within four weeks. The others were more difficult, as information flowed between the various Trade Union representatives. Careful language changes were made and small but irrelevant duty times and roster configurations altered, each enough to make the operating agreements unique to their operating area and yet still deliver the customer service package and as a consequence all rolled in on schedule.

The TS Operating Agreements were the start of a fine period of achievement (no modesty here) where all I touched turned to gold. While in this post, I achieved the first-ever annual wage award freeze in the company and went on to conduct three more negotiations where pay freezes at the annual review were accepted by industrial employees. Only one other such event ever occurred in the company between 1961 and 2002.

My old mate Graham Kendrick, now Managing Director of Courage Limited, sent me a letter of thanks for contribution to the business. It would have been great had he picked up the phone and said "well done Mike, let's have a meal together". Remember this was the guy who once told me I could not negotiate. However my "coup de grace" during this period was the replacement of the Reading DPS Agreement with the Reading customer service Agreement. These employees were like the Leyland car boys of the late 60s, the Liverpool dockers or the Heathrow baggage handlers. They had had everything their own way for twenty years.

Please read on and share my pleasure as I relive these particular moments of this one-off set of negotiations.

Oakley, the Regional Distribution Manager, once my Industrial Relations Manager at Berkshire you may recall, needed a new agreement as the customer service pressure, costs and unmanageable aspects of this particular depot were an embarrassing albatross for him. Plenty of conflict and many hours of argument here, and guess what the company are going to pay me for doing it? Oakley, however, could be like a maddening rash, never giving you a moment's peace. He wanted answers before he had even thought of the questions and to top it all his attention span was a maximum of ten minutes maybe twice a day.

Everyone would be nervous about these

negotiations. I would have to think of every "what if". In the extreme even the most senior director plays the game of I'll catch you out. It would seem to be some form of supernatural intelligence. I know we are all prone to the "what if" syndrome, but asking how you stop a parachutist from certain death when he jumps from a plane without his parachute is not really top of the class stuff for me. Nevertheless I would have to be prepared and if possible be diplomatic with my responses. You know how it goes, "that's a good question and I will have to consider all the ramifications before answering", knowing full well it would be asked. The questioner smiles and you give each person two minutes' air time. For now though I must put together my plan and a way forward. It will be slower than Oakley wants but hopefully deliver what he needs.

Among the many deviant practices that had developed was the 480-minute day (the eight-hour day they were contracted to work) which the crews had adopted an approach of demanding, particularly on a Friday but in reality on any day that took there fancy. The DPS Agreement allowed for an eleven-hour day (660 minutes). The net result was more work than there were men available or excessively late or wrong day deliveries as management sought to re-plan the work. Customers became increasingly irritated and trade management blamed distribution for loss of customers, falling beer sales and profit. The problems were actually more acute than this, as plans could not accurately produce pure 480s, often coming up short with 450 minutes, excessive numbers allowed on holiday at any one time and customer collections from the depot embargoed by the Stewards. Manpower levels had been established from the Bridge Street era which closed in 1979, but as I said modernisation of agreements was not a company forte and even when undertaken was not always directed at the real problems.

Equally confusing, the employees were guaranteed 40 hours per week and eight hours per day, which within the DPS Agreement gave the employees the best of both worlds. For instance employees who worked say six hours on Monday, Tuesday and Wednesday and 10 on Thursday and Friday actually worked 38 hours but received 44 hours' pay, the extra four being paid at time and one half, the 6 hour day automatically being made up to 8 in accordance with the Agreement. Incidentally there was a total ban on temporary labour in this depot, so there was no way management could alleviate labour shortage during the operational week by using external labour. They did so by begging and cajoling the willing and high earners into working very long hours.

I did a final review with the Depot Manager on the present bad practices and sat down to plan the way forward. Not much to tackle in the way of operating arrangements, there were five other depots using the same DPS Agreement, though none had gravitated to this state of restrictive practice, and some through good line management had opened up the agreement to make delivery far more flexible, though none of this was recorded.

After careful analyses of the current operation and matching wants of the sales fraternity and distribution management, I put forward a 27-point plan addressing the present bad practices, affording customers service to 9 pm, Saturday collections from the depot, Bank Holiday working (Easter only), provisions for the use of temporary labour, fleet loading and warehouse operating from work standards with job and finish as per the fleet/draymen, holiday rosters that related to numbers employed, normal seasonal breaks and trading conditions across those trading periods. There were three that I realized would not be achievable, such as a weekly guarantee of 40 hours only, rather than the current arrangements of both an eight-hour daily guarantee and 40-hour weekly guarantee, as these were enshrined in the Blue Book as part of the employee's substantive agreement or in simple terms, employee contract. It would be a fatal error to invoke Bargaining Unit involvement. These negotiations must be contained totally within Reading Depot. Despite this one issue, the rest gave me plenty of scope and I thought I might float this one. In any event, the Trade Union after all had to be able to kick something into touch.

The mismatch between daily and weekly guarantees would have to be wrapped up in the critical area of work allocation, thus avoiding lurches between issuing five hours one day and ten the next. The plan was designed to return control of the operation back to management, increase productivity, reduce costs by a minimum of £750,000 per annum (marginally ambitious), but the current costs were painfully high and made concerned reading for everyone. The savings had to be accompanied by high quality customer service which stood out among the brewers and still delivered the predicted savings.

Before negotiations began, we took all the draymen and warehousemen through a customer service awareness course using the sales team as major inputters. I did a number of dray accompaniments and participated in the deliveries and collection of empties, and in turn the draymen shared their sandwiches and coffee with me, occasionally having half a pint at the pub. They were all aware that after these customer service sessions the negotiations would start in earnest, and there was apprehension on the part of many employees.

Back down the road during the merger, we imported a new Personnel Director from the Grand Met merger, and he was proving to be a very nervous fellow, methodical in the extreme and highly dictatorial. To top it all the ex-convener appeared from the ashes of retirement to have his say, or so he thought. The MD of West and Wales was appalled at this latter development, but dear old Mr Kendrick had sanctioned a courtesy appraisal of management proposals for the ex-convener. It was rumoured but not confirmed that they belonged to the same masonic lodge. Unknown to me, the ex-convener had asked the new Personnel Director that I be removed as lead negotiator, offering the view that a new agreement had a better chance of going through without me, but this was refused. The ex-convener was right of course, because a totally watered-down version would have been much easier to negotiate, but as is often said this was not going to happen on my watch.

I took this man to a Hungry Horse pub, a carvery-type establishment. I write this without snobbery but it is worth noting he was accustomed to London's finest hotels and many of their restaurants and their most expensive meals, not to mention hampers from Harrods' for Christmas gifts, all at the expense of the company and all to the delight of his massive ego. I had no room for his ego, presence or principles. My action in choosing the drab Hungry Horse was deliberate. While I was not overtly hostile, the cordiality on my part was tepid and the overview of the 27-point plan vague. No key information was passed on, no help enlisted, no offer to keep him informed, no warmth offered to this man in whom I simply had no trust, whose principles were never ones I understood. He was someone whom I personally could never warm to. Oakley informed me that on the way home the ex-convener complained bitterly about the meal. That was when he told me he had asked for me to be removed from the negotiations.

Not only did I tell this man nothing, I reiterated all the bad practices that had been allowed to develop over the many years at Reading and for good measure I let him know I considered him personally responsible for many of the problems, nicely of course and with a well practiced smile to ease my venom towards him. Oakers flushed at this point. When the ex-convener had gone to the toilet I demanded of David Oakley that he should tell him absolutely nothing on the way home, emphasizing the poison between us and the danger to the negotiations access to the information would present.

The plan was finally signed off by the appropriate directors. I tiptoed through every element with immense care, not wanting to alert the directors to any weakness therein and sometimes stretching the truth thinner than cling film in-order to retain a point under severe scrutiny. The Personnel Director though was trying at every turn to handcuff my manoeuvrability at the negotiating table, a restraint which would make success very unlikely. As an individual my thought processes were heightened considerably as the adrenaline surged during negotiations. The more difficult, hostile and impossible the events of the negotiations became the quicker my thought processes became. Of course after a night's sleep I could not think how to get to the bathroom.

The Personnel Director continued to push for remote control from Head Office, and after many hours of separate debate with him, my boss and Oakers, it was agreed we would produce a separate note for the Personnel Director setting out our key response to areas considered to be of major sensitivity. It was at this point and for some light respite from the sheer pressure of Keith Allen's *modus operandi* that I allowed my mind to drift to another day, when Oakers turned up at my office with some important notes from a depot closure meeting that he had chaired.

David proceeded to unroll a scroll on which he had recorded important information about the closure of the depot and the Trade Union reaction. At about every third turn of the scroll it broke, fragmenting the words Oakers had written. He had recorded the minutes on bloody toilet paper, would you believe. Now I thought perhaps he might do the same with the summary for the Personnel Director.

My boss and Oakers were openly threatened by the Personnel Director in reference to the outcome and, yes, control of my behaviour and actions throughout the negotiations. This was a reference to the belief that I was overly independent and frequently operated beyond my authority. While this was often true, it may also have been related to the poison that the ex-convener had planted in the Personnel Director's mind. I was not privy to all the business plans, maybe Oakers and I had trod on a sensitive area. In recent months I had negotiated zero pay deals without the requisite authority. These deals had developed as an opportunity during negotiations and I took them in the belief that it was right for the company and business. On most occasions I was congratulated, but in the same breath I was often rebuked for stepping beyond my mandate.

Empowerment was the buzzword of the day, but individuals opting for such action were assigned to the loose-cannon brigade and labelled as unstable. There were times when the description fitted, though I considered most of my actions well judged and invariably well executed, no bias there then. Others were of course entitled to their views. The format now had been set and words would be written for the Personnel Director, who did not trust his own shadow to let him know what he was doing, unless written down of course.

As with every new Agreement, the "what if" brigade had been out in force. Oakley asked that I remain calm when addressing the depot management team; they had after all been under the cosh from the employees for nearly fourteen years. It was also of vital importance that this management team believed we could deliver. The meeting opened at 6.30 pm and lasted two hours. Maintaining a calm exterior was more exhausting than picking up every "what if" and dispatching them carefully to the dustbin, in such a way as to encourage belief in this depot team that we could succeed.

I had one or two advantages going my way. The new Convener wanted to make his mark. A new Agreement, particularly at Reading Depot, negotiated by him, would be a statement of his arrival on the scene, and we got on well. Moreover I had no reason not to trust this guy, unlike his predecessor. Oakley had the Transport Steward in his pocket. They had known one another for ten years, though the Steward was a canny fellow. These advantages would help and with the customer service awareness seminars now over it was time to get around the table and go head to head on the 27-point plan. Briefings for employees followed each set of negotiations in the early days and of course a debrief note for the Personnel Director and an hour's inquisition once he had read the note. The interrogation was supposed to have been via my boss, but the Personnel Director could not resist the direct approach and fancied himself in the cross examination role, tiresome, unavoidable, never challenging. The notes had been written in such a way as to make his questions very predictable.

The early weeks of the negotiations drifted and I was in a wave of annual pay reviews as far apart as Northampton and Swansea; five sets of negotiations, three different T & G Officials and extreme concentration was required on all fronts. We had now been at the table on seven occasions and there had been close to 50 hours of negotiation, explanation, tweaking, posturing and occasionally laughter, not to mention a few dockers' expletives. We were reaching a point where give and take were finely balanced. Oakley was showing signs of frustration and blew his top after an eight-hour session when I had refused to move one iota, denying every request for easement within the plan. Each item was being discussed, dissected and understood within the context of the Agreement, not in isolation. The Plan had never been put in front of the Trade Union; it had simply been wrapped up in the Operating Agreement.

The next step was to get acceptance of the principles of the plan through the Agreement. We had made much progress reference the principles and now it was more about who blinked first. David would clearly wish management to blink first.

I could tell in every bit of their body language, their eye contact, their voices, that when we met tomorrow we would be seeing the floodgates of acceptance open, but not today. Today I would only get half of what was needed. It was a fine judgement, instinctive, and it was about holding your nerve and optimising opportunity, but I felt confident. Tomorrow I would drop the 40-hour week demand and accept the current practice of a guaranteed eight-hour day and guaranteed 40-hour week. These would be the only concessions and they would be conceded only when I was absolutely sure all 25 of the remaining elements would be accepted by the Trade Union. The daily and weekly changes were quite frankly unachievable from the start as they were enshrined in the sacred Blue Book that governed the Bargaining Unit. I had however at the beginning of the negotiations spent an inordinate amount of time expressing the view that the language of the Blue Book was not absolute on these points. This was not true, but it kept the points on the table long enough to worry the Trade Union reps considerably. This would be a big win for them but of course, it was never going to be a loss for the company. For the company there was no damage in any way to the new customer service model or the return of operational control to the management team. Moreover I found some simple words about the Blue Book which covered the Substantive Agreements for Berkshire and all Courage Central Depots. These words were to be included in the new Agreement, giving the Convener peace of mind and a place to point his finger, if accused by others of selling the employees and Trade Union short.

It was my personal view that with the next day's give and take session complete and the notorious Blue Book protected, the money package could be concluded at our next meeting and a recommendation from the Trade Union gained. Everything should go very quickly now.

Then my boss rang to say that I could not at any time say that the excess employees would be made redundant; there would be a reduction of fifteen after the implementation of the new Agreement and they would form a significant part of the savings. On average they would be granted redundancy at £33,000 each. The instruction was hideous and illogical and would deal a death blow to the negotiations. In all projects of this nature voluntary redundancy was an accepted path to the savings and provided payback was available within five years was deemed to meet the criteria for redundancy and a commercially viable project. In this particular case payback was three years. This stupid stance might fit with a farce at the Old Vic, but this was a leading Brewer. The truth was that no one had expected the negotiations to progress so well (some probably thought I would fail some might have hoped). We were going through a merger and many London depots of the two companies were adjacent, so closures and redundancies were inevitable. Did that affect Reading or Reading impact on the London scenario? No was the simple answer, but someone fearful of their own shadow might think so. Keith Allen, the Personnel Director, thought he had resolved the issue by the avoidance of the word 'redundancy', rather like asking someone to sprint without using their legs. I was steaming.

There was no movement on the part of Keith Allen and the tedium of having to draft a response should the question arise (and it would) was quite frankly nauseating. Many hours were spent drafting and re-drafting the words to be used. When the question came in negotiations, I ignored the draft. It was far too long, and not being an actor I simply could not memorise its verbosity sufficiently well to sound convincing. My reply was simple. I told Alan Jones, the Convener, that the question of how we dealt with surplus employees was premature. We needed to conclude the Agreement, and then we would know exactly what we had in terms of surplus.

Alan was no fool and persisted by asking "So are you or are you not going to apply the normal procedures for redundancy? We already know we have surplus employees". I told him I could only repeat what I had said – "If you tell me you are going to accept our Agreement in its entirety then almost certainly I can estimate the precise surplus numbers but you are not going to say that, so at this time we are looking at an Agreement short of this and that will give a different answer."

Alan looked miffed but fortunately he let it go for the time being. Outside the negotiations I told him I could only deal with it once the Agreement had been voted in, but I would not let him down, though it would be helpful if he did not persist with asking the question. He responded in a very simple way by saying "The question will be asked until I have a satisfactory answer, I cannot let it go indefinitely". The Convener said he remained mystified as to why I simply could not give him the answer he expected, as we were going to have to deal with this before the agreement could be activated. I knew now how simple the solution would be, but timing was of the utmost importance.

The new Agreement was now in its final state. Only the money for the Structured Call Service at the pub, which included stillaging beer (putting it on racks) emergency delivery service and Saturday opening for customer collects had to be negotiated. Oakley had gone to Portugal to play golf. saying "You will walk it now Mike". However the redundancy issue was yet to be dealt with and the Warehouse Steward looked uncomfortable with his lot - I did not trust him to support the new Agreement.

The meeting to finalise the money and Agreement

went very well. Despite my concerns over the Warehouse Steward there was a unanimous recommendation from the Convener and Stewards. The redundancy issue was raised again by the Warehouse Steward and I side-stepped it. The Convener replied, we hear your answer.

Though the negotiations had gone really well, I could sense a ragged edge to everyone, people were nervous around me. I treated the Personnel Director with care and apologised profusely for my lack of verbatim redundancy response. The Personnel Director, though hacked off that his well chosen words had not been used, was satisfied that I had not compromised the company's position on redundancy. The Convener rang me an hour after negotiations had concluded and asked if he could run over some points with me before addressing the employees in the morning. I sensed a nervousness in his voice. I told him I would do it in the morning and meet him at 5 am (which meant leaving home at just after 4 am) to give us an hour plus before the employees started arriving. "Thanks very much" he replied, but I again sensed the nervousness.

It was now 9 pm and I started off for home arriving at 10 pm. When I rang the MD to brief him on the day's events his voice sounded odd. Perhaps I was becoming paranoid about how people were acting, but at the end of my phone call, he said "That's very interesting Mike, but you've got the wrong Martin". I must have been one digit wrong, but he did enjoy the debrief.

Finally I got the right Martin and he wished me luck in the morning and said he didn't think he would sleep easy. This surprised me, as he was a brash and ultra-confident sales guy from Yorkshire. He said the story on the street was that the negotiations would fail and the fallout would be that Reading Depot will become virtually inoperable. I felt a massive hostility and anger surge through my veins, not towards Martin but that bastard of an ex-convener, who I was sure had planted this story, not on the street but in the mind of the Personnel Director via his mate Graham Kendrick, and had probably been badgering the new Convener as well. "That story will be dead and buried by morning" I told him.

When Alan arrived the next morning he said his one problem was the redundancy issue. He said he needed to be able to say that the manning levels would be met via voluntary redundancy in the first instance. I told him I did not believe this would remain an issue for very long. We went over all the other aspects once more with me telling him exactly what to do in respect of the redundancies, hoping he understood, and Alan left my office at 5.55.

When he returned at 8.30 his sleeves were rolled up and his face was scarlet, but his eyes were shining bright. "We've got an Agreement" he proudly announced. The vote was 83 for and 13 against. But the employees would not go to work until the company guaranteed that the manpower reduction would be achieved through the normal process of voluntary redundancy and the redundancy terms were guaranteed as they currently stand. Alan had understood perfectly - the employees wanted their answer now and now we had an agreement pressure could be applied upwards, with success inevitable.

I thanked him and told him I did not have the authority to sanction what he asked for and could not request that we achieve the manpower via voluntary redundancies only, simply because if no one volunteered I could not achieve the required manning levels and the savings necessary to fund all the additional payments just agreed while delivering the necessary operational savings.

Alan replied that the company had to guarantee that the current redundancy package would apply as well as the current method of redundancy selection which allowed volunteers to go first, saying the employees would not go to work otherwise. "Right" I said, "Can you go back and explain very clearly what I am seeking authority for and try to get an undertaking that all today's deliveries, would be made regardless of the time it took me to sort this out. Five minutes later he returned with an acceptance of the terminology on the redundancies and a guarantee of all deliveries made today. I now had all the pressure points I needed to manage upwards.

When I rang the MD he was absolutely delighted, and I could feel his relief in every word he spoke. As word got out congratulations came in one after another. The Courage Board took until 11.30 to agree to the redundancies. The Personnel Director never said well done, nor for that matter did Graham Kendrick, but all the trade directors served by Reading depot were over the moon. Agreement to the redundancies should have taken five minutes. The draymen, to their credit, made every single delivery, even though it meant an 8 pm finish for some.

Six weeks later Courage announced 122 redundancies in London following the closures of two depots. Was it ever necessary to think that Reading redundancies might compromise the London announcement? Only men frightened of their own shadows could possibly think so. I worked with so many like that that at times it was like pushing water uphill with a rake.

For thirty years or more the Agreements had been the secret domain of personnel management and Trade Union hierarchy. This led to misinterpretation and myths which eventually became bad practices. To ensure such practices did not prevail again after the implementation of this Agreement, I decided to produce Agreements for every employee, so managers could offer to sit down with any employee and say "Show me where it says you can refuse to do this work". The Agreements were issued to the employees two weeks after the vote.

On the subject of individual Agreements, the deputy

fleet Steward stuttered quite badly and during the Customer Service Awareness Seminars had injected some humour into the sessions. The newly introduced 'structured call' required every dray crew to greet customers with a "Good morning" and offer to help stillage the beer in the cellar – simple, but not previously done. The deputy Steward had suggested that by the time he got his words out, the publican would have gone to open the pub for lunchtime drinks. I recall writing a one-page ode for him and inserting it in the front of his Agreement. He insisted that the Depot Manager read it to the rest of the depot guys. It was a simple thank you for the way he had conducted himself throughout the negotiations. His pleasure was immense, according to the Depot Manager.

Oakley was so delighted that he made arrangements to pay for Lorraine and me to have a fabulous weekend in a country hotel in Lincoln. The hotel was really upmarket, with personal waiter service throughout. Lorraine lapped it up and we were able to treat her sister and brother-in-law to a slap-up meal at zero cost. Dereck ate well - I mean remarkably well. On returning home Lorraine received a gigantic bouquet of flowers. The message read "Thanks for supporting Mike". The MD of West and Wales, Martin Loades, bought me a half of bitter, tight Yorkshireman you see.

Oakley now asked me to tackle the issues at Avonmouth. Plans were in place to extend the number of loading bays to accommodate the Ushers distribution work, which was currently undertaken at their Trowbridge depot. I was already in discussion with the T & G about its future, but we were not sure of timing in relation to the Avonmouth building programme. The Avonmouth depot became the second largest in the Courage UK operation and the current Agreement had now been in situ since 1981 with many obligatory tweaks since its introduction.

Avonmouth presented entirely different problems from Reading in terms of successfully bringing a set of negotiations to conclusion, not least because the employees of this depot had voted no to every annual pay review since it had opened in 1968. It had not been so important in the past, as the bargaining arrangements included other depots, processing plants and brewing, so the Avonmouth employees were nearly always outvoted. The Stewardship of the depot was not in strong hands, and the warehouse Stewards, though representing less than a quarter of the employees, were positively negative, and yes, I do mean positively negative.

One of the warehouse stewards practised being an 'asso' to the point of total success. The employees he represented were the world's greatest doomsday characters, who thrived on the suggestion of misery, doubt, disbelief and 'can't be done' with a never-ending diet of no's with regard to every proposal ever put forward. The saving grace was that they could quite simply be outvoted by the fleet.

There were many things in this agreement that had

common threads with the New Reading Agreement, but once again I used my trusted *Roget's Thesaurus* to insert as many different words for the same end product. I stylised the presentation to afford a look of originality. All money was allocated at different levels from those of Reading, being both higher and lower, albeit they had annual totals that were remarkably similar. Even holiday arrangements varied, and temp arrangements totally diverse. Keith Morris, the Operations Manager for Avonmouth Depot, of course had to swallow his pride as I would lead these negotiations, in which he participated very little, but he was frequently very difficult during adjournments and where we needed to amend to accommodate union pressure. In reality Keith was never a real obstacle, despite the difficulties he presented in adjournments. He did after all have a front to maintain in the company and in front of his subordinates, and in fairness was very complimentary about the content of the Agreement, sheepishly admitting it was a world away from his annualized hours effort.

The negotiations were endless. The meeting room was immediately below Keith's office and during adjournments we could hear tremendously heated arguments between the Full-Time Official and the warehouse Stewards in particular. However there comes a point when the negotiations reach a natural conclusion and the officer had indicated that the union were prepared to recommend the Agreement to the employees subject to one small amendment and a significant improvement in the money for the Customer Service Charter. We accommodated their requests, though for 'significant improvement' read 'reasonable'.

The vote was taken over three days and produced a rejection, albeit not significant - as I recall a 33 majority against, of which the warehouse employees probably contributed 25 no votes. I now stepped – or rather pole-vaulted - over the line of my authority, and without consulting the Personnel Director or for that matter anyone, I issued written notice of imposition, which included the appropriate month's notice to terminate their current Agreement with the company. That notice gave everyone the opportunity to think before acting. I had done this after consultation with the officer, who had said prior to the result of the ballot that if I issued notice of imposition he felt the workforce would not vote for a strike, but if they did he would have to support them.

I replied that I understood, but given this workforce's previous record it was an immense gamble. I had no managerial authority for my actions, but once taken the company had little option other than to support me. Not to have done so would have undermined all future negotiations with the Trade Union and confirmed their view that almost always the chief negotiator at the table had no authority to act. My job was on the line if the result went wrong. My problem was not the workforce but the management chain. The Personnel Director was totally silent as I relayed my actions. Oakley felt it had been a little rash. The MD West and Wales said "You get me into some scrapes, Mike!" and my direct boss said "You might not get out of this Mike". Another good day at the office then.

All four of us (my boss, Oakley, MD and me) were summoned to Staines, the Mecca of forward positive thinking and zero risk strategy. The Personnel Director had Julie O'Donoghue, Personnel Administration Manager, with him for the purpose of recording the discussions and edicts that might come out of the meeting. The meeting was opened by the Personnel Director, quoting Graham Kendrick and relaying his dissatisfaction with the events thus far. I listened but said very little in the early stages, being careful not to let my raw emotion out of the box over my disgust with yet another concern over the 'atomic rupture', as Keith Allen dramatically described it. The tirade, mostly aimed at me, was relentless.

There was a tiresomely repetitive examination of the current situation, then someone realised that I was saying very little and asked me for my views. I responded that the need to modernise our operations was not in question, we would have a ballot for strike action and even if they voted to strike that did not mean the Trade Union would call one. I said I believed the Officer's intention was to force the employees to take a real vote. They had nothing to lose by saying no as they had been doing for almost twenty years. The Avonmouth workforce had to stand on their own feet now, not hide behind others whom they allowed to say yes or no for them. This was the first time in nearly twenty years that they had had to stand up and be counted, and I believed they would remain seated.

I said that to rescind the imposition notice now would be like putting our weakest thoughts in neon lights; we had to play this out, and if there was a vote for strike action we would deal with it. Our best course was to do all in our power to engage the employees in discussion, showing absolutely no weakness.

Everyone turned to look at the Personnel Director. Eventually he said "We will let it run, but Michael, you will take no further provocative actions without consulting Steven [my boss] first, who will then consult with me and I will respond to any of your requests through him."

The last point was more about telling my boss to manage me than putting the handcuffs back on me during negotiations (after all that would have been like closing the stable door after the horse had bolted).

Oakers joined me for a pint after the meeting and congratulated me on my summary of the situation and my timing. Had I entered the endless 'what if' debate too early, I am sure my contribution would have been incoherent and laced with volcanic lava. Staying silent was very difficult, but timing was absolutely crucial.

Before the ballot I had had an evening meal at the Bowl Inn at Almondsbury with the Trade Union Official, just to make sure we knew exactly where we stood. I mention this only because in January of 2013 Lorraine and I had lunch there with James, Helen and Arthur. I was a most enjoyable lunch, but for a second or two the memories of many meetings and deals floated through my mind.

The strike ballot was very carefully worded and drawn up in accordance with the current legislation. The employees had been told that if there was not a vote for strike action, the officer would inform the company in writing that the Agreement had been accepted. The ballot was open for one week and one day to maximize the number of votes. Employees who were off sick were visited by Stewards at home. It was an agonising time. The vote was counted on the following Monday at 2.30 pm and the result was a complete reversal of the previous ballot, with a majority of 33 voting against strike action. Job done, but Keith Allen now considered me public enemy number one. Success sometimes has a whole series of unexpected consequences, but I enjoyed that vote and no one could take it away from me. Moreover, the guys in the depot now had much respect for my words and perhaps a little for me. Allen however would at the very earliest opportunity remove me from any role in personnel - talk about bitter-sweet success.

The company was now changing shape, and experimental business units, one in each trading region, were being set up. In essence they were built around the delivery area of the Distribution Depot and designed to sit very close to the customer base, headed up by a

Business Unit Director with three direct reports, Financial Director, Sales Director and General Manager Operations. They were deemed experimental, but they would be the future of Courage Limited.

Personnel's approach to this new set-up was to dismantle the Bargaining Units, these being a geographical mixture of many functions such as distribution, brewing, trunking fleets etc, whose main terms and conditions had historically been negotiated in a single group. Such ties did not lend themselves to the new regime. In the West and Wales, having spent the early part of my career cementing the Bargaining Unit together via job evaluation, I was tasked with dismantling it into its smallest parts.

I recall back in 1982 when I was promoted to Personnel Manager and attended my first Central Committee Meeting. They were held at this time in one of Imperial Tobacco's conference suites. Walking into the room, I was in awe of the scene in front of me. Forty Shop Stewards, twelve Line Managers, six full-time Trade Union Officials and of course two Site Personnel Managers, one from Bath Street Brewery (located at Bristol Bridge - originally George's Brewery) and the other Avonmouth Packaging Plant (built in 1968, now demolished). The Stewards were very casually dressed apart from the Newport man, who was booted and suited in some pretty expensive gear.

My boss chaired the meetings in those days and no other manager spoke unless invited to do so. While it was not quite as grand today as back then, I had possession of the chair, and oddly enough the Newport Steward (or more correctly Cwmbran Steward, since the closure of Newport Depot) was still present and still wearing the finest pinstripe suit and driving a Range Rover. The man even had racehorses, which were always draped in Courage blankets on race day. I digress momentarily, but Peter was an interesting Steward. One should not forget he was a humble lorry driver, yet he was a trumpet player and his wife headmistress of a Welsh primary school. Somewhere along the line he had inherited a bob or two.

I opened the meeting by welcoming everyone and went on to explain that over the next few months I would be exploring ways with the officers, Stewards and site management on how best we might consider aligning the bargaining arrangements with today's trading environment. Shop Stewards and employees are forever suspicious of management motives, but having got through the flak there was a general consensus of opinion that what had been presented made sense. The meeting agreed to go back to their sites and explain what had taken place and said they would report in one month on the concerns and what might be needed to go forward. It was a positive start to the unwinding of a near forty-year-old approach to collective bargaining within the company.

At the final meeting, when the procedures for separation had been agreed and I already knew my job was in jeopardy, I thanked everyone for their input over the years; many of the Stewards I had known and worked with for nearly fifteen years. The Trade Union officials in their response were one by one very complimentary in my direction. There were some wry smiles among the line management (not all) but there was also an echo of endorsement from the Stewards. In its way it was a sad moment and the end of an era. Many of the officers and indeed Stewards had helped me out in times of difficult negotiations, even when my own bosses were being a pain in the butt.

As I reflect for a while on this latest period in personnel, there is no effort on my part to exaggerate or distort, but in three years I had managed to negotiate more operating agreements than the rest of the company's personnel teams put together, a total of seven, affecting hundreds of employees. The only stoppage was a three-hour sit in at Reading Depot, while I waited for the gurus at HQ to agree to some redundancies. I had generated savings in excess of £2m, conducted 21 annual pay reviews, all accepted at first vote and three with zero pay increases, spent hours counselling salesmen who were losing their jobs as a result of the Grand Met merger, and not one Industrial Tribunal with regard to unfair selection. Now the merger was finished, Business Units were being rolled out and Personnel were going through their structure for the future - and guess what, there was to be no place for me in that structure.

It would seem that my efforts to deliver a high-quality contribution to the business and the balance sheet had been conducted in a manner that was unacceptable to the function in which I worked, or more appropriately to Keith Allen, the Personnel Director. Was my approach to success too coarse at the edges? And if so, was it really sufficient reason to exclude me effectively from the personnel function and possibly the company? The truth is, I was able to outsmart the Personnel Director too many times, and for him that was not acceptable. Moreover I had a severe and total objection to anyone telling me what to do, and quite frankly the careless way in which I dismissed my opponents and superiors had caught up with me.

Since the earliest days of joining personnel I had found it much easier to relate to and work with employees and most Trade Union officers than those of my peer group or the so-called élite of the boardroom. The former were after all, men and sometimes women drawn from my own plebeian background. These people were nearly always honourable, principled and straight-talking but never (as frequently portrayed) unintelligent, albeit educated. I found the attributes of the working man easy to identify with, starkly honest, sometimes childlike, often helpful, rarely Machiavellian, persons of simple pleasure. I liked to think I shared these traits. However with the senior management and directors my working relationship was never as easily established (though with some it was a close and profitable working relationship). With most I found duplicity ran amok. I did not take enough care when disagreeing with them to avoid bruising their inflated egos, and when their understanding was less than I thought it should be I delighted in mocking and them and outwitting them. This was not a recipe for harmonious working or promotional prospects.

My interview for a personnel post was not helped by the interviewer. I was interviewed by a spotty 32-year-old who had the favour of the Personnel Director and who was to get a major role in the new personnel structure - in fact he eased out my boss. This was a man whose skills related to writing policy documents under the direction of the Personnel Director in a format totally acceptable to his boss, not the cut and thrust of moving a company workforce forward. When he interviewed my boss's secretary for a job in the new structure, one of his questions was "How do you think you would cope in a strike situation?" Her response was "We've got Mike Boyd, we don't have strikes" (she told me this herself after the interview). She didn't get the job.

Keith Allen, I guess, did what many had done before and supported his man for the job. His appointee lasted less than six months in his new role. My approach was clearly far too full-on for Keith to manage.

I concluded my final set of negotiations as Employee Relations Manager in January 1994, the third of my zero pay deals, the Trade Union having withdrawn their claim following my request for a twenty percent reduction in earnings. Just a bluff you see, but body language and delivery can reward a wealth of achievement.

# CHAPTER SIX

# Operational management

That Christmas was made miserable by the thought of losing my job, and now I had to start the process of looking outside the company for work. Oakers suggested I apply for one of the general managers' jobs in Operations and said I would get his support without any problem. "Don't throw it all away now Mike" were his parting words. My boss grudgingly agreed that the Operations role was worth a shot, and on the day he was unintentionally helpful, as he hacked me off so much the adrenalin was really pumping when I went for the interview.

The applicants were from depot managers in West and Wales, plus displaced Grand Met distribution managers (their depots having closed) and Area Technical Service Managers. I brought up the rear from Personnel - a total of 21 applicants for 6 jobs. The MD

West and Wales chaired the interview and was supported by one of the other functional managers. The Regional Personnel Manager (my boss) joined the decision panel at the end. The problem for me was that even if I got a job I might well lose my senior management status, but at least it would pay the mortgage. I had done much research into the company trading position, as we were about to lose the "tie", where the brewer tied the tenants of their pubs to the brewers' beers/supplies. A very large number of pubs were being sold and the profit margins would be greatly reduced.

The interview was interesting. Many of the questions were Business Unit directed and there was a high emphasis on trade rather than distribution or technical services, which would be the key functions a successful applicant would manage. I was able to respond well and often with considerable accuracy in relation to these questions, such as the £1.4 million estimated loss in trading margins, and I sensed the MD was impressed. As the interview came to a close he asked what I thought was a rhetorical question with regard to my personnel status, saying I had presumably been given redundancy notice (I had not but I let it run) He asked me if I would consider becoming a transport or warehouse manager. The question had hardly left his lips when I said "Martin, can you really see me working for Ian Wilson? (currently a depot manager). Martin said "You see George, Mike's so confident in his own ability that there was not a moment's hesitation".

George told me later this one response, and my knowing the exact £1.4 million loss estimate, got me a very big yes from Martin.

I had to wait until the following afternoon to know whether or not I had been successful, when all those interviewed returned to Westward House (Regional HQ) to be told the results. I was quite confident of landing one of the jobs.

★ ★ ★ ★ ★

Even now as I write these memoirs the pleasure of being told that I had been one of the six successful applicants is still with me. What was more, to get the second largest operation in the company gave me a supercharged feeling. There was much activity, and Keith Morris, the departing Avonmouth Distribution manager, was first to offer his congratulations, good behaviour considering we had shared few positives together.

When everyone had left I sat and read the letter (I was based at Westward House so did not have to travel anywhere post the decision process). There was no salary increase, no change of management status, hurray for that. The letter did however carry a paragraph not found in any of the other appointments. It read "Your appointment is subject to a six-month trial period and should not be considered permanent until a successful completion of that trial". This inclusion bothered me not, I had never lacked confidence and considered it a reasonable inclusion given I was crossing functional disciplines and in reality had zero experience in the new function. I read once more the title - General Manager Operations. Two days later I was celebrating the news with our neighbours, and David Symes insisted on footing the bill.

It later transpired that before the appointment could be announced the selection panel had to seek approval from the Courage UK MD, Graham Kendrick, such was my reputation. It was thought I might be considered too volatile for this position. However Graham offered no objections and for that I thanked him, albeit in silence. This job was to bring my most enjoyable and influential period with the company.

The appointment of the Business Unit Director (BUD) for Courage West was one of the last to be made, which meant I had nearly six months without a direct boss - heaven, Shangri-La and peace all arriving at once. There was time to establish myself as I became involved in the regional trading meetings with all the new Business Unit directors in the absence of the Courage West BUD, great for the ego. On my first day in the job I recall walking up to the Depot as I had done hundreds of time in my training and personnel roles and thinking now that this was my site, and I would make it sing. I was welcomed by the receptionist and again by my secretary as I reached my office. There would eventually be brand new offices to accommodate the new management structure and office personnel for finance and pub trading, but for a while those staff would remain at Westward House.

On my first day in the job I arranged for a 4 pm meeting of my eight direct reports. They in turn each had some twenty-five reports, I never having had more than two previously. This meeting would remain a constant feature and would become known as the "Miners' Club", because it often finished in the dark.

There were a few objectives I had with regard to the meeting, the main one being to establish a new environment in which we would operate, but equally it was to admit to them that I had technical and basic functional gaps to fill in over the course of the next two months. In outlining the issues, I gently reminded them that my memory was my best asset and they should keep their responses full and honest as otherwise they might come back to haunt them - no keeping key elements up their sleeves. In terms of the learning curve I had for instance no knowledge of putting together budgets and the processes for getting them signed off. Stock management was a bit loose as well, despite my foray into the losses at Brooklands. Transport law was a fresh horizon and IT a nightmarish thing then, now and probably always.

For the moment I explained to the managers that I needed an overview, telling them I would catch up on the detail over the coming year (my own personal target being two months) and I made no apology for my lack of knowledge, saying they should not be embarrassed by the simplicity of my questions, as I would not be embarrassed asking them. There was, I said, another thing they should understand, that I expected total loyalty from them to me even when I was wrong, and in return I would reciprocate totally. Finally I said I expected them as managers to stand their corners. I want no yes-men.

We were off ,and these were to be good times, with the odd carbuncle, and bosses who thought they should manage me sometimes causing an odd hiccup. Many years after my retirement one of those managers present at that first meeting told me how on an afternoon when things might not have gone as well as expected, he would tell the latest crop of junior managers about a maverick Operations manager who had once been in charge of the  distribution depot who did it his way, a loose cannon who many thought was mad, you never quite knew where he would take you or where you were going or where you might end up but it was always a challenge and almost always exciting. For me this was someone's recall of my most enjoyable period at work. His conversation that day kicked my ego high into the sky and provided a retired man with much pleasure of a time past. I record this simply because I am proud that my approach to the job got a ticket of approval from my managers past, many years later. I recall saying to this manager at one of our ops meetings that his search for a new depot in Barnstaple seemed to be concentrating far too much on the Health and Safety requirements rather than those of distribution. "But Mike, we need a toilet" he protested. In my exasperated state I said "Look Clive, we need a distribution depot not a pissing depot". There was an outburst of laughter and we moved on.

The job was so much easier than the personnel role, simply because you had a defined task to manage and a direct management impact on that task. Personnel was often nebulous in functionality and often conducted via a myriad of people over whom you had little or no control. Nevertheless my experience would serve me well for the new challenge. With no direct boss in place, I went about the process of learning the nuts and bolts of the job. Most of my peer group looked only at the top levels of the operation, but I wanted to know all the boring detail. It would help with understanding the issues that arose and hopefully with providing solutions. Moreover my weekly operational meetings meant I was never more than a week behind a problem and often a month ahead. My respective peers rarely met with their managers, doing so only when a problem had grown out of control.

It was apparent however that my predecessor had left quite a lot of issues behind. Absenteeism was at 12%, a mistake of £100,000 had been made in the vehicle fuel budget, wages were 10% overspent and stock losses were running at £50/60k per annum (depot management were not quite sure of the actual figure). Large elements of the new agreement, particularly in the warehouse, had simply not been implemented. When I asked the warehouse managers why the latter had not happened they said it was impossible to measure a number of the activities, so the warehousemen were being given actual time taken rather than measured time. Stay with me please reader, the whole concept of the New Agreement was to encourage the workforce to perform at higher productivity rates. Actual time often meant the men worked slower in order to be paid overtime, thus earning more. The Agreement I had written was designed to allow them to work more quickly and efficiently and still earn good money.

I could at least tackle two of the problems immediately - namely absenteeism and the Warehouse Agreement, on both I was very switched on. At operational level, there was nothing I could do about the fuel cock-up. The budget had been set at a total spend of £10,000 and no one had noticed the error. The true spend was £110,000 and I would need to understand more about the stock before going head to head with the problem.

On the second day in the job I addressed the draymen and warehousemen at Avonmouth, many of whom knew me from the Agreement negotiations. I picked four specific elements in my opening address, the first being stock, telling them of the losses, and in the same breath saying as far as I was concerned everyone in the room was honest, and adding "Please don't prove me wrong". On absenteeism I indicated that I could not speak to those who were absent of course but I would be catching up with them and explaining that absenteeism that was genuine would be treated accordingly and absence that was a matter of convenience to the individual would also be treated accordingly.

I spoke also of the warehouse operation and finally of earnings, suggesting with honesty that my vision of the recently negotiated Agreement was of high customer service, high workforce output and high income. The latter was a surprise to them, and I was questioned closely as to whether or not I meant what I said. My answer was in the affirmative.

On the third day I addressed the Technical Services lads, suggesting we needed a new Operating Agreement. The current Agreement, with the exception of weekend working, had been in place since 1981 and was now very frayed at the edges. The technicians were averaging £28,500 pa when the average wage of this era was £19,000 pa, so there was an obvious need to sort it, as output certainly did not match earnings. I was to try unsuccessfully to negotiate a new Agreement some twenty months after moving into the job. It was called Tech 2000 and included a 30% hike in productivity and considerably more self-management by the Tech and was based on jobbing rates, which simply meant a time-over-money value had been established for every job and combination of jobs and then entered into a computer program to make it easily manageable. The program had been written by one of our former techs, a particularly bright bunch. Almost all had basic electrical or mechanical craftsmen qualifications and quite a number had substantial smallholdings, if that's not a contradiction.

There were many doubters among the management hierarchy and some dismissed Tech 2000 as no more than a 1960s piecework scheme whereby you got paid for what you produced. The technicians simply would not accept the concepts of Tech 2000, particularly those elements that required self management, and clearly the hike of 30% in productivity was proving a difficult pill to swallow. I would come back to this one later and continue for now to plan a strategy that would persuade the Techs that working with me was better than working against me.

Next up were the budgets. To be quite frank, I was all at sea with so many figures and apart from the workforce costs I had no handle on such things as the local business rates, vehicle depreciation and replacement costs. It went on and on. Eventually the budgets were pulled together, with Jackie Hayward, the Administration Manager, doing the work, but while the Technical Services budget got a tick first time round, I was told to cut the distribution budget by £150k. I was so mad that I deliberately cut items I knew we would overspend on and all were overspent in the following year. When questioned on this at later dates by the

Regional Finance Manager my response never varied: "they are the result of an enforced £150k budget reduction at the beginning of the financial year". This irritated the accountants and my new boss when he came on board. In reality we hit budget for 1994/95 with total savings of £125k, achieved by a considerable underspend on wages and a stock gain of £26k. That was Distribution - in Technical Services (T/S) we were underspent by £5k.

I had set myself some goals on settling into the job. One was to always achieve budgets, two was to have the lowest absenteeism rates in the company and number 3 was to encourage the highest level of productivity among the various group of workers in the company. Sadly, to achieve these goals I would need to change a number of my management team and reorganise the very flat structures that currently existed. Changing the structure would be alien to company policy, which had introduced the team management concept based on making managers directly responsible for their own teams. Good concept, poor application, at least at Avonmouth, and the managers at this site were as good overall as any elsewhere. My first experience of the problems with team managers was a brief given to the fleet employees (draymen) by three team managers all with the same brief which was translated differently, and even answers to the same question varied, not a recipe for success. Some managers were caught in a time warp, old fashioned chargehands in charge of a single operation. Some had been appointed to fill a gap with zero operational knowledge at basic ground level, others were in the wrong post and some were simply no good. The pressure to perform as a Business Unit was ever present and the fleet operation was wobbling a wee bit.

I was able to appoint an additional fleet manager, Diana Evans, who had worked with me in Personnel and undertaken a lot of training work in the Avonmouth Depot, so she was well known to the draymen. Within five months of her appointment she was to become my Senior Fleet Manager. Team managers remained in place by name, not responsibilities - those were rewritten and the name retained to avoid Personnel interference. Elsewhere in the company they continued in their confused state.

Very soon appraisal time had arrived. So had the Business Unit Director, but I will cover that later - he was after all only one of three and he lasted just twenty months. Appraisals had always been an emotional time for me and I wanted to be sure that my team had every opportunity to express themselves as freely as possible. Not all the appraisals would be good news. I lay bare my hostility towards the arena in which appraisals are conducted, often not against realistic objectives, frequently by favour not performance and under a forced distribution curve which applies to small sections of people who might all have performed exceptionally well or poorly, but still the curve is applied. The fairness of such a scheme is therefore doubtful from the outset and frequently damaging to morale and genuine performance. The whole of British industry and commerce is riddled with this sickness.

Ratings in the company were 1 to 5, 5 being low. Of my eight managers the ratings were 2x2, 5x3 ands 1x5. Generally speaking they met the curve, but I like to think they reflected the facts, not the curve.

When I had introduced the Staff Appraisal Scheme in Berkshire, I had insisted that there be an independent review committee of the ratings. I was, I admit, forced to accept the natural distribution curve of performance. The staff scheme was introduced into a heavily unionised group and unionised members sat on the auditing committee. A surprising number of assessments were amended. I recall one where a man had done no more than work excessive overtime, for which he was awarded a 1. The committee suggested this had nothing to do with quality of work and downgraded the assessment to a 3 on interviewing his manager. Not a perfect scenario, but at least the overseeing committee gave a backstop to fairness of application.

The appraisals I conducted were however well worthwhile and I sincerely hoped fair. A number of managers complained that I had on occasion been a wee bit abrasive, impatient, intolerant and had failed to listen - no holding back then. This I felt was good, because despite their observations, all totally accurate, they had no fear in expressing them - at least all bar one.

This guy arrived for his appraisal carrying a 450-page folder under his left arm. On his head was a hard hat and in his right hand a baseball bat. Before I could speak he said "Today Mike I am going to have my say. You will listen and when I've finished you can speak".

It was a very funny moment. I had rated him a three. I would like to tell you I upgraded him to a two. I did not, but I listened without interruption and when he left the office I am sure he felt as if he had been given a one - a good manager with plenty of balls, and I still receive a Christmas card from him every year.

After six months in the job I had restructured the management team, making one individual redundant, removing another from fleet management, transferring hard hat from warehouse to fleet and promoting a bright Stock Controller to Warehouse Manager. There were to be four more reorganisations during my time at Avonmouth. In between reorganising and getting used to having a boss around I was tackling the absenteeism. Two employees had not worked for 12 months. While it is not a breach of contract to be sick, failure to attend work for whatever reason does mean you are failing to fulfill your contract, which is tantamount to the same thing. We tackled the worst offenders first and moved on to those who stretched their sickness and then the annual two-week offenders. Eventually the absenteeism was down to 3%, with 35% of the workforce not taking a single day off. These individuals were rewarded with various promotional items scrounged from sales - T-shirts, umbrellas, special beer glasses, etc. The carrot and stick worked very well, yet not a single Operations Manager from other units came to look at what we were doing. We were however accused of massaging the figures - at times it could make you want to spit.

Interestingly, the father of one of Kirstie's friends who I had met at a barbecue and who worked for North Wilts Council was very keen to take on board the process, but not Courage Limited, a company which lost millions of pounds in absenteeism every year, one of the many frustrations working in a large company; it is immensely difficult to manage upwards. Almost all initiatives have to come down the line. Most of those coming down the line are copycat approaches in vogue at the time. They may excite the Board of Directors, but micro management of absenteeism does not fit this bill.

However, back to what I could influence. The management team was beginning to sing, and I was finding I had more and more time on my hands. The company had entered the world of Distribution Contracts as well as distributing to its own tied and free trade. All our own managed houses were sold off, a ridiculous decision driven by the parasitical city gurus who often knew very little about business and whose only ambition was to manipulate share prices, totally for their own personal gain. They were aided and abetted in this approach by the so called "Beer Orders" of the Monopolies Commission, a Government organisation which thought it knew how businesses should be run.

The £1.4 million loss in our region alone was due to this sell off and very large reductions in margins. Yes we pocketed some capital and our bottom line looked good for one year. In order to retain our supplies we became the chosen distributor to these newly sold-off pubs for five years, and eventually we sold all the tenanted houses, mostly with five-year attached distribution contracts, increasing evermore the number of contracts. David Oakley was to become the company day to day Distribution Director for this operation.

The first and biggest contract had been prepared on what the company thought we could achieve in terms of performance, not what we were actually achieving, and there were no clauses inserted that allowed the company a grace period to get up to speed, in fact penalty clauses were accepted for under performance on our part from day one at a level of performance we had never achieved. I could sense that the business acumen behind this contract was in-house and had served the company very poorly. Many years after its introduction Coopers Lybrand, a large City accounting firm, carried out an audit of the contract. The report might be described as reflective rather than heavily critical, but a number of the failings I had already identified appeared in their report. By a stroke of irony the lead Cooper Lybrands guy was Alan Moore, my old Personnel Director and mentor from my early days in Personnel. This first contract would be a disaster of some magnitude, but would eventually provide me with a perfect opportunity to march off into the sunset.

For now though, I set about meeting the requirements of the contract out of our Avonmouth Depot, even though some elements were hideous. There was simply no understanding of how we currently performed, and the contractual standards of performance were so high the company would never meet them, not just in my view but an absolute fact, demonstrated time and time again in the next five years as the company constantly failed to meet the agreed standards and paid huge sums of money in compensation for our failure - more about this later.

The new boss at Avonmouth was beginning to establish himself, and as is the Japanese way, Mark liked to dress in the same uniform as the draymen. My working relationship with him was mostly sound, but Mark was never really a people person and we did have a couple of brushes. The first was over a delivery crew which had upset our largest customer, or rather his wife. I was met by Mark and our Sales Director after returning from a trade visit to be informed that I must dismiss both draymen for their totally inappropriate behaviour at the account. On enquiring as to what this inappropriate behaviour was, I was told they had been rude. I knew the crew, they were rogues and they were lippy and had probably caught the landlady on a bad morning with a bad hangover. The Business Director said "Make no mistake Mike, they are to be dismissed." I quietly replied "I will look into the matter". Then I picked up the phone and asked Diana, our senior fleet manager, to pop up and see me. The Business Director said he wanted to talk to her as well. I said that was not sensible and left his office.

Diana arrived just a couple of minutes later, and I quickly ran through the issue. She said dismissal seemed unreasonable and I asked her to interview them quietly and give me her views. "If you think its just a bad-tempered or hungover landlady, we will need to dampen down the Business Unit Director's approach" I said.

Within the hour Diana had reported back that the lads had admitted to winding the landlady up a bit and that she had turned quite nasty and they were unable to recover the situation; it had been a joke gone wrong. It did not warrant dismissal or even disciplinary action. The following day the landlady was presented with a bunch of followers by one of the draymen and a box of chocolates by the other and the best apology any pair of rogues could muster. She rang Tony Bird, the Sales Director, to compliment the Courage West Business Unit on the quality of their draymen and the perfection of their apology. Charm is a wonderful thing. The Business United Director never mentioned the subject again.

For the third time since joining the company it was changing hands. This time the prospective owner was Scottish and Newcastle, a company Elders (Fosters) had tried to buy when they owned us. The Elders takeover had been blocked by the political might of Scottish Labour MPs. Scottish and Newcastle were a third of our size and had an ancient and draconian style of management whereby almost every decision was checked through almost to boardroom Level. The contrast with Courage was extreme, as we gave our business units considerable autonomy and provided close management contact with our customers. Scottish and Newcastle were strangled by functionality and hierarchial organisation, almost comparable with the Trade Unions' demarcation lines in shipbuilding back in the fifties and sixties when a carpenter did not dare to remove a bolt from a plank of wood to plane it but had to call a rivet man. In this company the exacting lines of management were very similar. Personnel were very powerful and no one stepped on their toes.

As with most takeovers, there was a period when the new company gauged its newly-purchased assets before integration began. There were many synergies in operations, as one might expect from two brewers getting together, more so in the North of England with brewing and distribution running carbon copy operations. In the south however S & N hardly existed, and Courage had no base in Scotland, so the takeover was felt less, though not in all areas. Brewing had some considerable overlap and at director level there was much duplication. I attended meeting after meeting where the S & N integration team spelt out the differences between their method of operating and ours. Theirs was claimed to be far superior, yet many practices were archaic and we had jettisoned such approaches many years before. This was going to be one hell of a challenge, given my disposition towards direct control from above.

One such meeting - or more a briefing - was with the Scottish and Newcastle Occupational Health Nurse for Courage, who rabbited on at length about the Access to Medical Reports Act 1988, with which I was very familiar, having written a "fool's guide" for Company Personnel Managers on its introduction. The spiel was quite inaccurate. Moreover S & N had produced a British Rail-like document that prescribed every rule and regulation possible for managing the Act, bound in a 300-page document. There was very little about how absenteeism and sickness might be managed. Employees of S & N had basically a 12-month entitlement before their absence could or would be tackled in the workplace - wonderful for the genuine, utopian for the malingerer, hopeless for the manager trying to get to grips with absenteeism. Having listened to the Occupational Nurse for twenty minutes, I finally challenged her interpretation of the Act, saying that what she was saying was incorrect and access to employee records was not confined to the medical or personnel function only. She flushed and blurted out that it was S & N Policy. I asked how a line manager could act correctly towards a absent individual without knowing the individual's state of health. Her reply was typical of the S & N approach. She said medical and personnel would know and in any event, no action was taken for at least 12 months.

I reminded her that there was no employment law

that prevented an employer from doing so. I told her that at Courage sickness benefit entitlement ranged from 10 to 26 weeks, so even if we were following the S & N approach decisions had to made much earlier than she was indicating. Moreover, to wait until sickness benefit was exhausted before taking action was a dereliction of management duty and unfair to the individual, and many Industrial Tribunals would deem this to be poor management behaviour. It was the first of many challenges with regard to the wisdom of S & N Policy.

In between picking up the challenges of the S & N takeover and our darling Occupational Health Nurse, I was asked to chair a Disciplinary Hearing at Stage 4 with the potential of a dismissal on conclusion, at our Plymouth Depot, which was managed by Mr Smith, the Operations Manager. This was one of our new Business Units and the Director had asked through Personnel that I handle the case. I have to confess that I did not get on very well with this particular Ops Manager and questioned whether I was the right person for this particular task. My old mates back at Personnel were clear that I should take the chair, as was Paul Hoffman, the Business Unit Director, whom I had known for many years. We tolerated one another, no more no less. I send "Hard Hat", the man with the baseball bat, to do the investigation. The Personnel Manager complained about his style and something rude Hard Hat had said in the heat of the moment to the Ops Manager. I had learnt years ago how to deal with such accusations. I responded by saying Clive would not have said that. People don't know what to say when you use such a line - they can't argue with you and they can't make any headway with their complaint, particular when dealing with an encounter on a one-to-one basis, ie between accuser and accused. It was a tack I used many times to protect my errant managers, I said he would not have said it at least four times.

The Personnel Manager gave up and moved on to how the hearing would be handled. I told him I could see no grounds for discipline, let alone dismissal, and that I believed the accused was a misfit in the Depot, having transferred from Technical Services, and was finding it very difficult to fit into the culture of this Depot, a culture in which a fellow manager could report him to his Ops Manager simply because he was having a conversation about the Depot's possible closure with one of our salesmen in the privacy of his own office. This was no different I said from you or me speculating about the future of a director discreetly over a coffee in your office. The Business Unit Director should have put this to bed before the Ops Manager got on his nasty bike and suspended the man. I suggested that he should go and see the Business Unit Director and lay out the facts. I would play no part in rubber-stamping the Operations Manager's nasty management style. Sean asked if we could do the hearing and discussion with the BUD on the same day.

Driving to Plymouth, it was clear to me that no

matter how much I disliked Smith's style of management, our solution would have to allow for his ego. On arrival I summarised my position, reiterating that I did not think discipline was warranted, let alone dismissal, and suggesting that to protect Smith's position, I should pen a strongly-worded letter about gossiping in the office. The Business Unit Director was silent. Smith was outraged, face scarlet, barely able to utter words coherently. He thumped the cabinet, saying this man should be sacked, he was a disgrace to the Depot and could not be trusted among the men. He stepped forward and I was sure he was minded to belt me one, and Sean spoke sharply to him about being rational. I left the room to let them sort it out. I returned with the letter and the Business Unit Director and Personnel Manager read it. Smith would not even look at. They both said it was fine.

The hearing was conducted as a full Stage 4 hearing with the possibility of dismissal. The Business Unit's Secretary was present to take verbatim minutes and the man was represented by Gareth Evans, sales trainer with our company and formerly with Grand Met, as was the accused man. Gareth was a feisty bugger throughout the hearing. I concluded the hearing by saying "Your choice of conversation with a colleague was perhaps ill advised and I shall communicate to you separately on this. With regard to the alleged disciplinary offence, I can find no reason to take any disciplinary action."

The words had hardly left my mouth when the

secretary punched the air with her fist, shouting "Yes yes yes!" The accused visibly came back to life and Gareth said "I knew we would be all right when I was told Mike Boyd would be chairing the meeting, I knew we would get a fair hearing". I said thank you and told the man he was free to return to work as normal. Two months later he got a job in sales, and his purgatory was over.

My next challenge to the S & N style of management came with a further confrontation with my dear friend the Occupational Health Nurse, who visited the Avonmouth site to carry out some routine tests for fork lift truck drivers and sent two men home because she considered them too poorly to work (bad headache and a right stinker of a cold). The nurse had not informed any member of my management team and neither of the guys had complained about their health at the start of work or during the course of the morning. I informed the Business Unit Director and the local Personnel Manager that I could not let this go. Having spent nearly two years creating an ethos among the employees that real illness only would be tolerated, a headache and a runny nose coupled with a power-crazy nurse was not going to deflect me now.

I wrote to her boss, a doctor whose name I forget, stating that the nurse's approach was intolerable, inappropriate and her actions beyond her powers of authority. I wanted to be able to argue on as many fronts as possible. If the doctor suggested her actions were within her power, I wanted to know at what level the authority had been invested and where within S & N policy documents such a statement was made and under what circumstances it could be acted upon. If no such policy giving such authority existed, then of course it would never happen again on one of my sites. If such authority did exist then I wanted to make it very difficult to enact. If it did not I would pursue an immediate apology. A policy that permitted such an autocratic approach had to be reined in and therefore I would attack in the strongest possible way and among the widest possible audience the way in which such action was taken and the effects upon the management team and indeed the employees' it could totally change attitude their to attending work and managers of managing such events.

The saga ran for several months, with me becoming increasingly embroiled in weekly and sometimes daily rows with the S & N doctor, but eventually I got my way. Moreover all medical reports were seen by me and no one else was sent home by the Occupational Nurse, nor did she ever visit one of my sites again. When a new doctor arrived in the South I was able to coax him into writing more meaningful reports and working very closely with line management.

Works doctors are notoriously vague with their reports, simply because they know they may be used to suspend or stop sick pay, read by the individual, the diagnosis potentially challenged and the report and the doctor exposed at Industrial Tribunals, and from there into the newspapers. The latter would be very rare, but if you are a practising doctor you need to take very careful care of your reputation.

The medical challenge was one of many. Some irritated, others were a pleasure to pursue, but to know your enemies is always wise; some are not as obvious as you may first think. My old mate Keith Allen was still Personnel Director, but even less sure of himself now S & N had taken over. The local Personnel Manager for the area was Sean Jennings, whom I had known and worked with for nearly 20 years on and off. He twisted the knife when I had yet another confrontation with Allen, this time over a disciplinary decision related to the absenteeism of the warehouse Shop Steward, whose alleged sickness had become an issue over several months. He was already on a first written warning for absenteeism and was now given a second. The disciplinary system allowed for four such warnings before dismissal and the tot-up method had to relate to offences of a similar nature. It was entirely possible to have several written warnings at different stages on unrelated matters. In fact this individual was on a final warning for careless driving of a forklift. The current disciplinary action, followed an alleged bout of food poisoning caused by a rogue canteen sausage, his fifth absence in as many months. Following the second warning the Steward wrote to the Employee Relations Director at S & N complaining about the disciplinary action for being sick.

It is worth noting here that his own Trade Union

would not support his appeal – it is very rare for a Steward not to be supported (fellow employees no doubt had informed his Union Officer that he deserved what he got given most of the Depot had eaten sausages from the same batch with no ill effects) but dear old Mr Allen wanted the decision rescinded, under pressure from the Employee Relations Director, his new boss and a man operating in a 30-year-old time warp. Sean Jennings informed Mr Allen early in the discussions that he had advised me that taking action against the Steward was not wise. The truth was he advised me after the event, not before, but clearly he was trying to score Brownie points with his boss and not in any way trying to help me. I would not forget his actions. I had known Sean for nearly 20 years and we had been close working colleagues for many of those years, but he already knew which way my old mate the Personnel Director was going and was happy to twist the knife.

I was being ordered to rescind my manager's disciplinary decision. If I refused then it was made clear I would be suspended for refusing to accept a reasonable instruction, especially as I had been advised by personnel in the shape of Sean Jennings not to take the action in the first place. I could have argued Sean's actual recollection of events but could tell he was not for changing. I could refuse to change the decision, but I would be suspended and forced to resign and someone else would change the decision - not a lot of fun or gain down that route. While my boss supported me the best he could and his anger with the outcome was obvious from his face, he was not going to make a difference on this one. If I rescinded the decision then all our work on absenteeism would be once again in jeopardy and the kudos gained by the Steward would be unbearable. The warning was on his record for nine months. The disciplinary had taken place two months earlier. Having argued about the damage to our work on absenteeism a rescinding of the action would do and reminded all present that neither the Trade Union nor the employees were offering any support, I proposed the following. The decision to discipline would be upheld, but instead of the warning staying live for nine months it would be live for only two months, and as this time had already passed the warning would be deemed to have been completed.

There was an acceptance that the proposed action was an acceptable way forward. No one asked about removing it from his record, so it was not. No one instructed me on how to convey it, and it was conveyed in such a way that the Steward was fearful of having his discipline increased. The disciplinary action was never rescinded, never removed from his record and never talked about by the Steward again. It had been a near disaster for me, but I smiled about my slight of hand for many months afterwards. The Steward's bouts of sickness returned to zero for the rest of my time at the Depot.

There was to be one more battle with Keith Allen, this time over Tech 2000. My new boss was very keen to relaunch this Agreement. There were savings of £1.5

million (Western Area), largely from reduced personnel and vehicles. It also provided high-quality customer service, a key requisite of my boss. The Technical Services Steward had come to see me to say that the techs were finally prepared to talk to me about Tech 2000. I had for two years squeezed their earnings, given them notice on their agreement and imposed a single-page contract from which we had managed and which they had worked to. It had been difficult. Their Full Time Officer had wanted them to ballot for strike action, but the technicians had not. Now we all had a chance to profit. The first stop was a presentation to Keith Allen, who had already seen the presentation in its fullest form, so all of us were taken by surprise when Keith reacted less than favourably.

The Agreement had been presented to the Personnel Director, the MDs of Courage West and Wales and Courage Eastern, the latter being very interested in finding a way forward with technicians in London. He was considering tapping into the proposed Agreement for his Technical Services Operation. The presentation at that time had taken me one and half hours with every "what if" carefully rehearsed beforehand and every positive point magnified within the presentation. There was immense interest from Des, the Courage Eastern MD, and Martin, the West MD, and the Trade directors of both regions were very keen on the proposals, as they impacted so positively on customer service. They were however concerned over the negotiability of the Agreement.

To my amazement in stepped the Personnel Director, who said, and I quote, "I have seen Mike negotiate some remarkable Agreements. Were anyone else presenting this Agreement I would be doubtful ,but I am confident Mike will succeed". I was taken aback, but the go-ahead was given. Unfortunately I could not bring the bacon home first time around - the Techs had not been ready, now they were.

I was presenting to the same people less Des and his Trade Director but including the Technical Services General Manager Courage. I had simplified the presentation and presented in headline statement fashion with little explanation as all present were totally conversant with the content of the Agreement, savings, customer service advantages and the fact that the Trade Union were making positive overtures. The presentation took less than 20 minutes. On completion Keith Allen exploded, quite why I'll never know, but I suspect he was under tremendous pressure from the S & N personnel camp to keep a cap on any events that might rock the boat in terms of negotiations with the Trade Unions, with whom the S & N fraternity were trying to establish a working relationship in terms of their new takeover.

The Personnel Director let forth. "Michael, that was one of the most immature presentations I have ever witnessed" he said. "Here we are examining a proposal that will have to go before the S & N Policies Committee and Central Personnel for approval and you present as if it is a Sunday school nursery rhyme. This simply will not do, it will not do at all". There was passion in his outrage the likes of which I had never seen. There were looks of shock, not only on my face but on everyone's other than the Technical Services GM, who had obviously been primed to give me the most difficult time possible.

Keith Allen had momentarily thrown me with his passionate dismissal of my presentation and I was pretty hacked off when the Technical Services GM asked me a loaded question aimed at embarrassing me. My response was aimed totally at embarrassing the GM. I said "It is difficult to take the question seriously when the GM for TS is totally aware of the answer. If you've forgotten the answer I'll go through it again, but I did go through this point with you yesterday on the phone" (a lie). I gambled that he simply could not remember every issue we covered and the stupid question had been a plant from Keith Allen.

Allen was in like a shot. "This simply will not do Michael. If you persist in this attitude we will close the meeting down and that will be that." Help was at hand from my boss, who quietly asked Allen what was necessary to take the Agreement forward. The Personnel Director suggested I sit with the Technical Services GM and prepare a paper for the purposes of this committee and that in the first instant it should be appraised by those present. When all present were happy the General Manager TS Courage Limited and I would consider its presentation to the S & N Policies

Committee and Central Personnel to view its potential and possible sign-off. There were clearly many things wrong with this approach. The Techs and Trade Union were keen to move forward now. The Technical Services GM would do exactly what Keith Allen told to him to do and committees, as the Government demonstrates daily, are a device to delay any decision for as long as is deemed necessary. For me also was the real risk that the content of the Agreement would be so diluted or distorted that it would no longer represent a meaningful way forward.

This was not for me. I would have to accept the so-called committee route for now as not to do so would simply mean an end to any progress. Somewhere there was a way round this impasse, but I was certain it was not in this room nor with any of those present. For the moment I would engage the Courage GM with mock and earnest debate on the way forward and let him lay a false impression with my mate Allen that I had fallen for the committee route. I worked hard with the Courage GM for Technical Services, but I put forward seemingly impossible solutions which he duly fed back to Mr Allen, only for Mr Allen to reject each proposal, as was the intention of course. However a way forward was beginning to emerge in my head.

I had earlier in the year been part of a management development team drawn from Courage/S & N management to look at ways of bringing together the two teams of Courage/S & N to the best advantage of the new company. I had an instant solution, but you could not sack all the S & N management team. The committee membership did have one advantage; I had met a number of senior management in the S & N Company including Gordon Rae, Senior Personnel Manager Operations (early 30s ex schoolteacher) and we struck up a good relationship, both being fanatical football fans with very good memories for footballing facts. It's surprising what makes a working relationship tick. He was to become a very important ally in the Tech 2000 scenario.

Now I turned to my old mate David Oakley and explained what had happened and the fact that I needed to make the right kind of contact with someone in S & N who was functionally responsible for technical services on a daily basis, someone who could make or influence decisions at the highest level relating to the implementation of Tech 2000 Agreement and someone who wanted to demonstrate to the Courage fraternity that he had power. "I know the man Mike" he said, "but I will have to test out whether or not he is up for pushing on with your Agreement or willing to give you a hearing." I told him that if he could get me a hearing I would do the rest.

Two weeks later David told me he had spoken to Jim O'Neil, Director of Technical Services Operations for S & N, and he would be ringing me reference the proposed Agreement/meeting. It was another week before his secretary rang to say she had Mr O'Neil on the phone for me. The call went well and it was agreed that I and the Business Unit Director would fly to Scotland to present the basis of Tech 2000 and take it from there. We would leave it to the respective secretaries to sort out the date.

I quickly informed the MD of my plans. He was very cautious about my approach and distanced himself from my actions. I did not know what had been said between him and the Personnel Director but clearly he was uncomfortable. I endeavoured to reassure him that this was purely a functional route and did not impinge on Keith Allen's committee, although such a committee might become defunct if I could swing it via Scotland, which of course was my key objective. The MD washed his hands of the scenario I painted, saying "I cannot support or become involved in this Mike, if you and the Business Unit Director (BUD) wish to explore this route, you do so of your own volition and without my knowledge. The Personnel Director will react accordingly, so be very careful and good luck". I relayed the conversation to my boss and suggested he kept this one within the Business Unit in case we were kicked into touch before we got started. He frowned but raised no objections.

The flight to Edinburgh was my first ever flight, at the age of 49 (my grandchildren started flying around three years of age). The usual plane had broken down and was replaced with a prop propelled plane that looked like something from a 1930s movie. The pilot was separated from the passengers by a curtain and luggage was stored in a section of the plane next to the passenger seats, rather like a double-decker bus from the sixties, where you placed your luggage under the stairwell before taking your seat upstairs. The flight time was one hour and ten minutes normally, but we were an hour late taking off and the plane was blown backwards by strong head winds and took one hour forty five minutes. I was convinced at one stage that we were being overtaken by seagulls. The meeting was scheduled for 10.30 am and we arrived just after 2 pm. Great start, and my ears were so bad I could hardly hear anyone speak.

Jim welcomed us to his office and had sandwiches and coffee laid on. His hospitality was superb and our preamble prior to the presentation was very much exploratory in terms of personal careers and Jim's position in the company and what he hoped to achieve. In terms of the presentation and picking up the questions on the operating and technical side, that was very much left with me. My boss covered customer service and the Business Unit ethos. I sensed an interest, and a desire on Jim's part to demonstrate his position of power and influence in the company. I was irked only by his reference to piecework mentality being embodied in the agreement. I praised him for picking out that element but said there were many subtle differences which took it far beyond the 60s piecework environment and the approach of that time. Jim went through a list of items that he would like to see covered off and he had major concerns about the quality of work if a piecework-type scheme was to be introduced. He said that when employees were paid for output rather than time there was a tendency to cut corners and the quality of work suffered.

Jim said he wanted to talk to Robin Holmes, main board Personnel Director (Allen's boss's boss) and suggest that we work together as a team to launch this as an "alternative experiment" alongside other initiatives in Technical Services. We both nodded enthusiastically. Jim asked who we would like as the personnel guy to ride shotgun, as there had to be a personnel overrider on board - this was the S & N way. I nominated Gordon Rae (I had only had one conversation with him and that was mostly about football, but there you go). "That would be a perfect choice" said Jim, "I know him very well, used to work for me".

My boss was very happy with the outcome of the meeting and I sensed a certain admiration with the way I had handled matters. In truth Jim was keen to play this one out and establish his credentials among the Courage fraternity and for once, I had been ultra cautious with responses and my presentation content. With the green light given by Robin Holmes to explore, and if satisfied a sign-off of Tech 2000, we were up and running. A meeting was arranged to present the new Agreement and pay structure.

Four weeks later my boss, Jim, Gordon and Keith Allen's number two, Martin Beecroft, met at Jury's hotel in Bristol. Why Keith chose not to be present is interesting only to me, but I believe he was on his way out. Once more I had out-manoeuvred him and he would have been to embarrassed by my presence, the reason for his absence however was more likely the former. The evening meeting was no more than an informal get-together and a chance to enjoy a few beers and a decent meal before the main event the following morning.

It was an interesting meeting, and Jim and I stayed up to 4 am. Jim drank heavily as I fetched the drinks from the bar, mine being lemonade and Jim's gin and tonic. We had many, and in the process formed a good working relationship that lasted as long we both remained at the company. The following morning our meeting went really well and we got the go ahead to negotiate the Tech 2000 Agreement.

The Agreement was unique, yet it was only ever implemented in areas where I had control or significant influence. In truth no more than 25% of Scottish and Newcastle adopted the Agreement and its presence in the North and Scotland was zero. It was unique in that it gave 40% more productivity than any other operational agreement within the company and scored similarly against external companies. Wages on the other hand were no more than 9% higher than the norm for this type of work and customer service was rated the highest in the brewing industry (again judged externally). Technicians had to guarantee their own work, ie go back and put a job right without pay if their work was faulty (which covered the worry of piecework mentality). Such a clause had never been negotiated within a Trade Union environment before or probably since, and it prompted the newly-appointed Managing Director of Courage to question its legality (rather than applaud its audacity). The task was carried out by 33% fewer men (geography prevented equal productivity gain and manpower reduction). The technicians also uniquely and frequently made their own working arrangements with publicans, even working through the night to complete the work (personnel management and senior directors in this era talked much about empowerment - well, this was real empowerment). It was, without modesty, a remarkable Agreement, and for me one of my finest achievements during my working life.

The company however continued to allow 75% of its technicians to be paid for completely inefficient methods of operations at very high cost and low customer service levels, rather like the NHS of today, sadly. The estimations of annual savings, had this Agreement been applied throughout S & N, were in excess of £20 million a year. None are so deaf as those that do not wish not to hear. As I have said elsewhere it is nigh impossible to manage company strategy upwards, and to this end I was a complete failure. Our industry since the latter days of the industrial revolution has become ever more riddled with champion ditherers. Even now as I recall Tech 2000, anger rages very quickly with in me over the ineptness of much of British management.

I am lucky to have been able to implement such an Agreement, to have had the help of one ex-mechanical fitter and one ex-technician (both later becoming managers) in the compilation of a work matrix that formed the basis of the contract between technicians and the company, and be blessed I guess with the savvy to know what makes the working man tick and to know he or she is blessed with the same motivation as everyone else, namely a desire to earn good money, enjoy their work and do so with a degree of independence. These desires are of course the same regardless of the sphere in which you work. Most management gurus and the UK's leading men of commerce and industry fail to recognise these traits among their employees, but with incredible self deceit are ready to fill their own pockets with outlandishly simple-to-achieve bonuses, which are rarely based on actual performance. Perhaps that's why they have no concept of how their employees would wish to be treated or motivated.

Nonetheless the above period was one of my most satisfying times at work. I had gone round the Personnel Director, produced half a million pounds in savings and picked up a couple of influential contacts in a highly positive manner. The technicians who worked for me had to a large degree stepped from a highly-managed routine into one of self determination in how much they earned, how hard they worked and with a new-found status to their job, I considered it a nice day's work.

One year after the Agreement had been negotiated, Keith Allen left the company, to be replaced by Gordon Rae.

Now we were back to the humdrum business of the Annual Review of Terms and Conditions (T&Cs). This story, ironically, is about the Techs' annual review. My mandate for the negotiations had to follow the strictly laid-down S & N format and be signed off by both Courage and S & N executive committees. The Tech 2000 Agreement had delivered all that had been asked of it, including the £500k saving. Avonmouth and Barnstaple were not in Western Area. The going rate for the year was at or around 3%, and I had obtained a maximum 4% mandate based on the improvements of the first year. I thought that was that, but as we approached the final conclusions to the negotiations, the 'shotgun rider' for Personnel, Julie O'Donoghue, insisted that I had only a 3.5% mandate. I was close to going mental. This was an outstanding bunch of techs, 40% more productive than any others in the company, and now I was being told I could not settle at the mandate level I believed was available. What was more I had already told the Full Time Union Official that we would finish at 4%, which he was very happy about, as it was a full percentage point above most recent settlements. Yet here we were again applying blanket awards regardless of employees' efforts and flexibilities.

The 3.5 was the same for every group regardless - what a load of bollocks.

First I had to alert the officer to the development, explaining at the same time how I hoped to get round it. He said he wished he had known before as everyone was now focused on the 4% target. I promised I would try to find a way round the problem.

The Courage Employee Relations Manager was unmoved about the ambiguity of his memo and would not countenance any movement, so I spoke to his boss, Gordon. The 3.5% would be the basic rate headline settlement, but I proposed that because of the gains we were achieving I would upgrade the matrix rates by 4% to recompense and maintain the technicians' super performance. Gordon said this was no problem provided the headline 3.5% was not breached and the additional half a percent on basic was clearly recorded as productivity gain.

Not for the first time in these negotiations, my next move would not have withstood quality investigation, but knowledge of Technical Services performance and costings were only understood when they got into the millions and as a consequence the Technical Services budget nationwide was grossly overspent on frequent occasions. The matrix was uploaded with a near 1.75% increase, simply because I was so hacked off at being told I could not move forward on what I considered a reasonable and justifiable basis. Only my team would know. Julie would be clueless and so would the Courage

Employee Relations Manager and indeed the S & N hierarchy - far too much detail, you see.

I explained to the Full-Time Official, who was happy with the switch, then we went over it with the technicians. The Stewards were careful, but indicated without setting off the alarm bells that they considered the matrix upgrade as extremely fair and hoped the balance of work delivered the 4% that management had indicated. They knew it was rich. The deal went through without a problem and cost £20K more than it would have done had we settled at a straight 4% on basic rate and matrix. I felt a childish sense of 'up yours' and when I next spoke to Martin a desire to take the mickey, but he would not know why.

# The last round

The company was moving on. The S & N influence was taking shape and the Business Units set up by Courage Limited were being merged and ultimately heading for oblivion. It was a tough time for management, as most Units which were largely based on a single distribution depot would now be based on 3 units in some cases and even more difficult for the 12 senior management/director posts were being reduced or regraded significantly. In the case of the West and Wales Operation I was to take control of Wales Distribution and Technical Services along with the Technical Services in the South West, while retaining control of the same functions in Avonmouth and Barnstaple.

There was however an issue over my salary. I told the Business Unit Director that I could not accept the new role based on the money offered. His consternation was a pleasure to witness (we had had a torrid relationship since he took over from my boss of Japanese experience). By this time I was 52 years of age and in any redundancy situation would be entitled to a pension. I had seen the salaries available for these changes (through a deliberate secretarial slip) and knew my boss was not being fair to me. He looked at me with surprise and anger, not quite understanding my opportunistic statement. He took to repeating himself in his frustration with my stance, and warned me I could lose my job. "Yes Simon" I said. "But you and the company expect me to reshape Wales, close depots, create new operating methods and negotiate agreements where Personnel have failed on three occasions and you want me to do it on the cheap. It' a no go. Surely there must be a remuneration upgrade package for these changes?"

There was a long silence, with angry eye contact the only communication. Then I suggested a solution. In two weeks' time the annual appraisals were due. I said I would like a guaranteed rating of 1 (the highest) and a salary increase of 15% on top of the miserly increase being offered today of 2.9%. That would take me to a level of salary that I would find acceptable for the job - not outstanding but reasonable.

He told me that such a rating could not be achieved before I accepted the job. I said I believed him to be an honorable man (there was a softening of his expression, though not the eyes) and would trust him to deliver the rating and the increase. He was no slouch with figures and quickly worked out my target figure. "Fine" he said. Could I trust him? I was not sure, but he did deliver and in the same appraisal year the MD for West and Wales

(Charles Williamson, an ex Bristol City professional footballer and S & N's replacement for Martin Loades) wrote some enjoyable comments about my contribution to the company. I was to work quite closely with Charles in the latter days of my employment with the company.

With the salary issued sorted, my attentions were turned to Wales. I had enjoyed my times working there as an Employee Relations Manager and would be going back to meet some genuinely decent colleagues among the draymen, techs and warehousemen, staff and management. One of them would be Pete Heal, the well booted and suited shop steward-cum-racehorse owner, who following one meeting in Wales had accused me of cruelty to his dog. On enquiring how this was he said "You made me so mad at yesterday's meeting that I went home and kicked the dog". However in the years that had passed, Newport, Cwmbran, Cardiff, Bridgend and Whitland depots had all been closed; only Swansea and Caerphilly now remained, the latter being an S & N depot built partly on marshland and now sinking back into the mud. The former was an ex-Grand Met Depot. The Caerphilly depot would have to close with Swansea expanded and Avonmouth taking over the rest of the South Wales delivery operation. There was much work to be done and a very stubborn S & N workforce to deal with. Bring 'em on, I thought.

\* \* \* \* \*

Throughout these working years, my children had grown up without too many misadventures. I was so absorbed with work that much of my children's upbringing was Lorraine's domain. She had taught James and Scott to read and write before they started school, and now suddenly my daughter would be entering her final year at university. As I approached the changes in Wales, I recall the day we had dropped her off at her lodgings two years before. It had felt very strange and uncomfortable to go off and leave her on her own.

When Scott's turn came he was twenty, having switched from Lackham College to Plymouth University for his degree. That was less dramatic. We shook hands and I said to Lorraine he would have some good adventures.

James we saw off twice, once for Reading (where he lasted one day, or was that one afternoon), then took a year out and settled for Cardiff University, where I think we tried to book him into an all-girls' hall but James of course already had a partner and was therefore rather more independent so there was again no concern. There is a photo of James on our study wall aged five, taken by his headmaster, and it is a perfect picture of total application. As he seeks his doctorate (James was successful in May 2013) that dedication is still apparent. Of course, now I have much more time to enjoy my children, now in or approaching their thirties. They can be a pain in the butt occasionally and they are full of their own opinions - and guess what, not all coincide with my own.

★ ★ ★ ★ ★

Returning to the work environment, for the next year and a half I was to spend much time in Wales preparing the ground for the key changes to our distribution operation there. However I had also gained a degree of influence in the Technical Services function across the company, and while I failed to get Tech 2000 adopted across the firm, the stats produced by its implementation in the West Country were unavoidable. The productivity, cost and customer service ratings were so good that senior management and directors were intrigued by them, even if at times they simply disbelieved them.

I spent much of my time away from the now enlarged Business Unit, presenting to MDs in London, the Midlands, Lancashire and Scotland. Human Resources used me as a sounding board or even an arbiter over costings, productivity levels, practicalities of new schemes when were put forward.

You know your influence is real when the Managing Director of Courage Limited invites you to join him for lunch to discuss a problem in the Midlands.

"The problem I have, Mike, is that my Business Unit Director has put forward new proposals for Technical Services and Human Resources have categorically refused to sign them off, based on your assessment of the costs and earnings potential." The MD was of course a friend of the BUD from way back. "I would like you to back off Mike if that's possible" he said.

This was a sign of real influence, but equally a new and different problem. If I said I could not do that I made a real enemy, but if I said it was no problem the agreement would be a disaster. In the end I backed off with a caveat note to Human Resources to monitor closely the earnings over productivity and to avoid any copycat Agreements. Charles was happy and our working relationship took a step upward, as he was my boss's boss, which would be useful if I had to call in a favour later.

While I was dabbling in the affairs of Technical Services, I was coming to terms with the operation in Wales. David Williams, the General Manager for Operations, now reported to me rather than a Director. It was a kick in the teeth for him, and others across the country were in the same position. Before he joined my operational team meeting for the first time, I told my managers he was to be given the very same respect they gave me and failing to do so would mean they were in deep trouble. I have to say my team were really marvellous, providing David with some comfort over the next eighteen months.

That period was to see success and failure on the distribution front. While sizing up the Welsh operation I was writing a new Agreement for Avonmouth Distribution, for a totally modern almost 24/7 operation. In the background the company was planning a nationwide approach along the same lines, but it would be a while before this came to the fore and almost certainly a fudge when it did so. It would be aimed at putting the operation in a state of readiness for selling off, in my view. This was always denied by the directorate, though it was obvious nevertheless and ultimately would come to pass.

The new Agreement provided seven-day cover for 16 hours a day at point of delivery and 20 hours a day at warehouse operating level. It was the most complete service envelope anywhere in the brewing industry. The MD was smitten with it and the company gave it a green light almost without hesitation, vetting its cost-effectiveness via an accountant and a central distribution guru after I refused to complete the complex authorisation process necessary for cost validations and group sign-off. The money I had requested was exceptionally high (in fact the Steward, in response to the deputy fleet Steward's question as to how it would be paid replied "in a fucking wheelbarrow I would think".

Negotiations had been very lengthy, with massive hurdles to overcome with regard to the employees' objections. The employee camp however was becoming quite split, and while negotiations were going well it was obvious the Warehouse Stewards were saying yes and meaning no. The Fleet Stewards were saying yes and meaning yes, but they still had to carry their colleagues with them - not easy.

In Wales we were ready to announce the way forward. The plan included the closure of Caerphilly, the expansion of Swansea and the setting up of a stockless depot in Cardiff (vehicles loaded and parked ready to deliver the next day), all to be announced 14 months ahead of actual closure. To maintain quality of work, and equally important, attendance at Caerphilly, I proposed that a two-year pay deal be struck whereby employees would receive the whole of year two's increase but only work for two months of the second year. The only sting in the tail would be a daily deduction for every day of absence between the day the deal was struck and the day the depot closed.

Negotiations at Swansea on a new Agreement would take place without the presence of any of the Caerphilly employees. Should they subsequently wish to transfer they would take up the prevailing Terms and Conditions. With the announcements of closure, negotiations started the following day at Caerphilly and were concluded that day with a full recommendation from Stewards and the Full Time Official. It was rare indeed for this officer to have a firm stance on anything, but the Stewards were very strong characters and true leaders of men.

I presented it to the men as a done deal and they had little spirit for a fight. The one obstacle was the strict application of no attendance no pay. In the extreme this meant that someone who missed 10 months' work over the next 14 months would not receive any of the additional 10 months' pay for the second year pay deal. Of course no one in any event would be working, but the plan was to prevent large and uncontrolled absenteeism leading up to the closure, always an issue at a closing depot. The argument was put to me in simple terms – "I break my leg, I am off work for 10 months, therefore I receive no extra pay, that's not fair". I had had this debate with my management colleagues ad nauseam. There could be no acceptable variant to the rule that every day off was deductible. In my response I explained that the extra 10 months' pay was for 100% attendance and nothing else. It was a genuine attempt by the company to reward those who helped out the company. After all the individual with a broken leg would under the terms of the S & N sickness scheme receive full pay for 10 months, the same pay as his mate who worked for the 14 months without a day's absence. "I believe that is absolutely fair" I said. "You are rewarded via a high quality sickness scheme and your mate is rewarded via high quality attendance".

There were small murmurings of acceptance and we moved on. Their spirit, as I said before, was low - they had after all just been told their depot was closing and only a handful would keep their jobs. Acceptance was reached in less than half an hour. As a footnote, absenteeism for the 14 months was less than half of one per cent.

My job now was to keep this depot going in good

order until closure and move on to Swansea and strike a deal there. The Avonmouth negotiations slowed on announcement of the Wales restructure, as the employees rightly considered their own positions had been strengthened.

In Swansea there was of course delight with the news of their retention as an operating unit. There were no natural leaders among the men and the Trade Union Official (ex Bristol City centre forward Terry Bush) would not be helpful. He would not lead only hinder. I decided it would be easier to commence and conclude negotiations with the entire group of workers plus their Trade Union Official. There was of course some huffing and puffing from Head Office personnel, but the objections were overcome as I stretched the truth and agreed to caveats that I had no intention of following during the course of negotiations.

The new agreement was based as always on working very hard and high earnings. The company benefits would come from very high productivity and quality customer service. There were approximately 30 people working in the depot, a small one, but it would increase by 50% under the new distribution configuration. The meeting would commence at 3.30 pm, post completion of work. The negotiations were actually marvellously good natured, often comical, downright noisy and then deadly serious. The Officer was particularly difficult, deliberately offering no guidance, but this was normal for him. I could see the body language, sense the warmth when we were close to agreement and the hostility when we were not. I could pick out the individual detractors and whether or not they could or would influence the outcome and go for their jugular if they proved influential. Had they been in the mess room waiting for the Officer and Stewards to report back, no such opportunity would be available.

At 7.30 pm some of the lads were becoming very twitchy, primarily because they were worried about getting home late for tea, but they also realised they were going to have make a decision. The Agreement was simplicity itself - more tons delivered by the fleet, more money, in the warehouse fewer men to move tonnage through the warehouse, more money. What actually would happen in the warehouse was that the same number of men would move 50% more tonnage -their decision, not mine.

One of the employees asked if we could go home and start again tomorrow. My response was careful. I knew that if the deal was not made tonight it would not be made at all. The men would invent a hundred reasons to procrastinate and the officer would blame the forum in which the negotiations were being conducted, not to mention our Group Employee Relations Manager saying I told you so. The sour ones among the employees would go into overdrive to put irremovable doubts into everyone's mind. We could stop now, but I believed we were very close to a conclusion. I suggested we take a five minute pee and smoke break and said I would then push on to a conclusion.

In the recess I asked Andy Poole, Regional Personnel Manager, if he would stress that in order for me to put the final offer on the table the employees needed to give an indication of their goodwill towards the concepts and offer being made. I needed a basic acceptance in principle, a tried and tested route forward. I had to know what the consensus of feeling was. I needed to watch the faces of the influencers, their hands, their eye movements, any indication that helped me know when the right moment to triple the offer had arrived. I knew there would only be one moment. I also said to our fast-track management trainee who was assigned to me as part of her development to come and sit by me and expose as much of her legs as possible in order to relax the minds of the lads. Was this sexist? Almost certainly, but my desire to get an agreement was the only reason for the request. I hoped the shop floor lads would be well distracted.

Incidentally the previous week I had given her a rollicking about her attire. She was an absolute stunner and unknown to her, I was going to make her part of the implementing team in the next phase of negotiations. There was a smile, and she said "Will this do?" I replied that I certainly believed it would.

Andy picked up the restart, and I watched every single face. Most listened intently to him as he made his plea. Few failed to glance at those legs and eventually one or two muttered their basic interest in the deal. If I got this right I had a real chance of a successful conclusion.

"It's late lads" I said. "I am going to make you an offer now that will significantly improve your earnings and as an added bonus my colleague Ms Bell will be a key member of the implementing team." There was light-hearted approval and the announcement broke the tension. I detailed the offer slowly and deliberately. I sensed a receptiveness and moved quickly to take a vote.

A single piece of A4 paper was issued to each employee and they retired to the mess room to take their vote at 8.30 pm At 8.40 they returned and the officer handed me the folded vote papers. They looked relaxed. The vote was 29 in favour, 1 against - we had a deal.

It gave me a wonderful feeling of elation, and my reputation as negotiator was sky high. My boss rang at 9 pm just as I was driving off from the depot, his voice betraying incredulity at the speed and success of the negotiations. The street odds on a one-off deal in the early evening after work were 250/1 against. Do I boast? You bet I do. That day I had left home at 6 am, walked into my office at 6.45, prepared all the details of the negotiations, rehearsed for several hours every set of figures, every what-if, timing and the amounts of money to be tabled, and I would be arriving home at approximately 11 pm, job done.

Now I had been invited to join the Technical Services Strategy Group, the only non-director to participate, and I was travelling to Newcastle and Edinburgh weekly, but I was beginning to sense that this project was doomed. The disparity between the four operating groups was unbelievable. The groups were Scotland, Newcastle and North East, John Smiths and Courage. As I took on board the differences I was confronted by the four operations directors, who were interested only in defending their own empires. Some were pompous, all bar one very intelligent, and most simply didn't like me, or as my boss put it, "They are not fans of yours Mike". I was already aware as I gathered comparative performance stats that none matched those in the normal circulation of the company. The directors were producing reports that matched the company format but gave no real indication of the ineffectiveness of their technicians or their incredibly poor management of stockholdings. I knew already that my contribution would be smothered. It would be too damaging, when one tech in the company was getting £10 for a job and another £50 to do precisely the same job. Anarchy and inherent incompetence were apportioned in abundance. Stocking holdings were showing tenfold differences for almost identical operations. These were the things I discovered, but I could not find a way to bring it out into the open in the forum in which I was operating, and the more I dug, the greater the issues.

I suggest that it was entirely possible to save between £15m and £20m per annum on direct operating costs, ie wages, employment costs, vehicles etc, and £30m one-off stock recovery over five years. There was a sense of incredulity among the group I was working with (nearly all of whom were director status) when I rolled out the figures.

A month after tabling these figures the strategy group was reconfigured and my name was not included. The directors had closed ranks. As I said earlier, for a fleeting moment, I was in the frame to take up the position of National Director, and this was some 18 months after my name had been quietly removed from the strategy makers' list. The odds of it happening though were at best a hundred to one. Too many enemies, too many small minds and too much knowledge.

★ ★ ★ ★ ★

Working life, as I said previously, had some moments of pleasure, and on the odd occasion I met a celebrity. At a Courage-sponsored boxing event I was lucky enough to chat with the great British boxer Henry Cooper, and on another occasion Lorraine and I met Steve Davis, six times world snooker champion. We gathered his autograph for the mother-in-law, who was a massive fan. At the Copthorne Hotel in Newcastle, I had breakfast with the Governor of the Bank of England, Eddie George (well to be honest he was sitting on the next table). Lorraine and I bumped into Bill Roache (Ken Barlow of Coronation Street) in Bristol and exchanged pleasantries, I dined with several Lord Mayors of Bristol, but they were so famous I cannot recall their names.

On another occasion, at a senior management team building session, I shared a few cigarettes and an everyday chat with Jon Pertwee, of Worzel Gummidge and Doctor Who fame.

Now back to the more humble surroundings of Avonmouth. The new Agreement was proving very difficult to deliver. The camp was split down the middle and the odd thinking among the men was aptly demonstrated by Richard Pickett, who had relatively short service at five years. At 20 years' service he would be entitled to £400, so this payment was being made 15 years early and immediately consolidated into his customer service payment. It meant Richard would gain considerably over the next 15 years to the tune of £4500 on this one element alone, but not only was he adamant that I was giving him his own money but that because of it he would vote no. However much his manager and I explained the sums he simply would not listen. It was a vote we should not have lost. Others voted no because they thought it wrong that employees with just five years' service would get the same as those with 20 years. Every employee was given an individual breakdown of their increases. Some would get as much as £3500 pa, not bad on an average income of £20,500, and this was 1999/2000 with a different work ethic.

I sat in my office waiting for the ballot box to be delivered via the Stewards: Dave Woodington, ex-Army and a dead straight decent guy, senior Steward and advocate of the Agreement, and Dave Ackerman, a six foot five ex-doorman who was totally against the Agreement. They arrived at about 2.30 pm. The box was opened and papers assembled in piles, yes to the right, no to the left. There were no spoilt papers. The two piles had moved at a roughly equal pace and now looked very even. Ackerman counted the yes votes, Woodington the no votes. The yes votes totalled 62, the no votes 65. I showed not a hint of emotion.

Dave Woodington was gutted, while Dave Ackerman could barely hide his delight. I rang Martin Beecroft, Group Employee Relations, with the result. You're home and dry Mike" he said. I did not comment, as I did not share his view. I then rang Paul Swain, the Full-Time Trade Union Officer, who had done his utmost to get the Agreement accepted, and he voiced his disappointment.

The decision by Dave Woodington not to allow those who were known to want redundancy to vote almost certainly affected the result, suggested Paul. Probably, I said, but the ballot for industrial action in which they were allowed a vote suggested otherwise. Paul decided there and then to have a ballot for industrial action. If the employees did not vote for strike action then the Agreement would be signed by default. If they did decide to vote for industrial action then he would lead them in strike action if the company attempted to enforce the Agreement.

The Electoral Reform Group would run the ballot in accordance with current employment law governing such ballots. The result was a disaster, with a vote by a majority of 7 for strike action. The company, with its bigger strategy to pursue (preparation for sell-off of Distribution, although this was several years away) decided that it was not the right time to have a punch-up with the Trade Union and I would have to back down and find a less contentious solution.

This had been an Agreement so rich in cash for the workforce that I had never believed the company would sign it off. It did, but the lads thought only for milliseconds before denying themselves a pocket of money for high output and high quality service, with the inconvenience of working bank holidays and one in twelve weekends and once in six weeks an evening roster to 10 pm.

Twenty-four months later this group of workers was forced to accept a very similar set of working conditions for nothing, outvoted by other employees in a regional vote. Their earnings were protected for 18 months and at the end of that, distribution was sold off. Today I believe their earnings are less than or equivalent to those of 1999/2000. It only demonstrates the foolishness of those who only really wanted to say no because they could. The freedom to shape your own future can sometimes provide a bitter reward.

With the Technical Services snub still to the forefront of my mind and now the failure to get the Avonmouth Agreement through, my ego had taken one big bruising. A simplistic way out for the Avonmouth

Agreement was found with only differential rates retained. There was little scope left in the job and the company was changing rapidly. The Business Unit's autonomy was clearly going to be abandoned. The operational functions of Distribution and Technical Services would be managed nationally, not immediately but certainly in 2-3 years.

The question now was what to do next. I was 53 and wanted out. I was tired of being at odds with the company, tired of an unequal fight against directors whose self-serving objectives made working life a pain and aware that my own style and desire to drive my ideas through the malaise that was the company's managerial and strategic structure were now failing.

The future looked grim - until one more break came my way. The MD of Courage Limited asked me to take on a key role in managing the distribution contracts within Courage Limited, which covered the West Midlands, London, Kent, South Wales and the West of England, including London West, a gigantic distribution depot which had been opened three years previous and had never operated properly but was responsible for 50% of the SSL (pub group) contract deliveries and was failing day after day, as were many depots, but not quite to the same extent or with quite the same impact.

The job was really that of a troubleshooter. It was a sideways move, not a promotion, but I did get a 12% pay increase after much persuasion by the MD and Personnel Director, Gordon Rae, who drove down from Staines to see me personally. Gordon's advice was simple. "Mike, we have worked together for some time and I know you can smell the changes ahead, you would definitely not enjoy the future if you were to stay in the current job. In fact your current job will not exist in its present form and in reality nor will the troubleshooter's job."

He told me I would be given a way out. I said I would take the job and thanked him for his candour. My reading of the situation was that two years from now S & N's reorganisation of Operations and the company would mean my job would be gone. How long it would take to sell off Distribution and Technical Services I could not estimate, but I would be free to take redundancy, as no appropriate alternative would be available.

Operations Manager was the job title, contract management the role. I recall that on one occasion I had to instruct Distribution Managers to go their local supermarket and buy bottles of Smirnoff Red Label Vodka on expenses for onward distribution to SSL customers, ie the retailers' pubs we were contracted to supply. There had been a total disconnect between Marketing, Waverley (our wines and spirit division) and Distribution. This was a business making £430m per annum with a turnover in the billions, but the contract was so badly written and our own internal organisation so disjointed that needs must applied. I met with resistance, not surprisingly, from some of the managers over whom I had no authority, but my powers of persuasion were well honed after years in personnel and when I rang the last and 17th manager on my list at 9.30 in the evening, in my car on the way home and only just past Reading with another hour's drive, he said, "I'm not doing it Mike, it is bloody ridiculous, foolish nonsense, and anyway I am at home". I said I agreed wholeheartedly, but it would be even more foolish to be the only manager to refuse.

Of course the major problem with delivering the contract in the South of England was a mega depot based in West London just five miles from the Wembley Stadium. London West Depot proved a nightmare, and continuously failed to meet the distribution contract by a mile. A 30% failure rate was normal. I approached this problem the same as all others, identify first the causes, then examining possible solutions, assessing the practical impact of implementing those solutions and finally making recommendations to the appropriate directors. My direct reports did a fabulous job in identifying the root causes of failure and we produced a 'Red Book' with 15 key recommendations, all accepted and implemented. Sounds grand, but in truth all the recommendations were basic sound commonsense distribution principles. We just bound them nicely in a red folder and presented them as work in need of urgent progress, with no criticism of the incumbent management. Your solutions are often more welcome down this route, as managers are not distracted by having to defend themselves and are therefore more receptive to your recommendations.

After 18 months in this troubleshooter post, with some successes but little pleasure, the company announced major changes to its operation. The net effect was that I was able to engineer my redundancy and a reasonable pension. Making it through to 55 years of age meant no reductions on the Courage element of my pension.

My retirement in January 2002 completed my service with the company. Almost twenty-three years had passed. I failed to make a good retirement speech - speeches were never my forte, though I made many in my career. When I reflect on those years however, it is with some pleasure in terms of what I achieved with what I had at my disposal. My level of education had been lean and my basic intelligence rather second division. In terms of education I had every chance, but you cannot get out what is not there. Nevertheless I was lucky to find roles where I could debate with vigour (something I really enjoyed) and one in which, I discovered, I had an innate instinct for understanding the behavioural traits of the workforces and the individual talents of the people I managed. Moreover my desire to understand and enjoy the minutiae often paid real dividends at operational level and again in debate. I also like to think my deep sense of right and wrong was very helpful. All these elements combined, alongside a high opinion of my own opinion, to enable me to punch way above my weight for most of my career.

In negotiations and everyday conversation I was always as interested in the body language as the words that were being spoken. Intuitively I could see a yes when I was hearing a no, or vice versa. It was, I think a little unusual. My own pride with regard to my achievements is always with me, no doubt a little exaggerated viewed through those tinted glasses, but not too much, I hope.

# Taking it easy

As I take a second check of those memories and life at work, I often think back to those working days, prompted by today's events. I can match the vast pay of directors and bankers with many of the men with whom I worked, some of whom I considered parasitical piranhas, particularly at boardroom level. Is there a tinge of envy? No - a tinge of bitterness maybe. I gave so much, but my return financially was never equal to those boardroom charlatans. An ordinary man can expect no more I guess, unless of course he measures his return in doing things the way he wishes to do them.

Retirement meant we had money, and were in the black with not a single debt. We had salted a little away from the sale of Lorraine's house in Ramsgate. In the intervening years the money had come and gone; we had not managed it well. We had a mortgage of course, some nasty credit card debts and up to my retirement we had lived from month to month. The package I received however allowed us to pay off the mortgage, the credit card debts and buy the company car which I had got new at Christmas 2000 and still have today some 11 years later with mileage in excess of 150,000. We still had some money left over to do the many jobs needed at 243 Quemerford. To think it had taken 39 years of work to get out of debt. Well, it was worth the wait of course.

The pension I was to receive was a bit below par. 22 years had not quite been long enough to provide a reasonable pension, even though for the last five years of my employment I had contributed an additional £5k a year through a small tax avoidance scheme. This was addressed through the augmentation of my redundancy (paid into my pension, again avoiding 40% tax) and I took a tax-free lump sum from my pension, so I actually paid in more than I took out. Thus today we have a pension that for the moment, and without debts or mortgage, provides a reasonable income.

What next? Well an advert in the local Gazette asking "What's your garden worth?" would dictate some of my early retirement. Our neighbours had put in for planning permission for four bungalows but had quite deliberately not involved us, so we went ahead and contacted the company who had placed the advert, Curtis Mayfield, and they came to visit. They were very interested in the site and equally interested in the neighbours' planning application. When their application failed I informed Curtis Mayfield, who then made contact with them, setting up a meeting in

Marlborough when they made each of us an offer in secrecy so no one knew what the other was being offered. Divide and conquer comes to mind. Six months had elapsed since my retirement and all our plans for 243 Quemerford were put on hold as we digested the offer for our land.

Then out of the blue a call came from the Operations Director of Courage. They wanted to take me back to work, initially for a month, ultimately for five months. Given that we were waiting to sell, the DIY work and revamp of the garden were put on hold and this opportunity fitted perfectly. I had to close a depot (the manager had been dismissed) in 28 days, which would save the company £250k in rental costs, and set up a temporary operation out of Berkshire Brewery while Hays completed the building of a super distribution unit at Thatcham. I was offered the same salary as I had retired on and all travel expenses to and from work, plus any others incurred during the course of the assignment. It was a no brainer, but it reminded me very quickly why I had retired. There is little doubt that I could have remained on contract for at least a year, but while it was a nice interlude, I yearned for the simple side of life and after five months, I returned to retirement.

In the meantime, progress of a kind was taking place on the land sale. Our own offer was not acceptable and I needed to know what the others were being offered, so I suggested we meet and have a discussion. Andy and Faith, our immediate neighbours, hosted the session in their garden. Andy had been a Squadron Leader in the RAF and was recently retired, Barry was a Captain in the Army, also retired, Ken a gardener and Karl a general builder. Only Faith of the ladies was still working; her vocation was as a freelance reporter for local radio.

The meeting progressed slowly, but at an opportune moment, I did suggest that we each needed to know what the other was being offered. Access to the site would be via ours and the neighbours' drive, which put us at some advantage in terms of the overall share. The other issue was the value of our properties, as we both wanted to sell. Eventually I kicked off with the offer which had been made to us and each neighbour reluctantly followed suit. It was apparent to me that we had not been given a fair offer in comparison to our immediate neighbour and certainly Ken and his wife were getting a raw deal. When next the houses were to be valued, I suggested that to ensure correct share levels and value of access we measure the ground being made available by each participant and a rough cut estimate of access. Then a second meeting with Curtis Mayfield could be arranged where we would look for an improved offer.

Barry made contact with Swallow Developments and Wilson Homes, and Barry and I would meet them to see what is on offer. Barry and Andy measured the ground and I prepared a matrix so we could instantly evaluate the offers. The access was set at 20% of the total land offer, split two thirds for us, one third for Andy and Faith. In truth it should have been 75/25, but we felt generous in anticipation of a good payday.

We met with Curtis Mayfield on three more occasions. By now they had met quite separately with our neighbours on the other side, the Sunderlands, Sims and Woodmans. Paul Woodman, who is a personal friend of our solicitor, came to see me to see what was going on and he told me a week later that all the other neighbours had had a substantial offer, his being a nearly a quarter of a million (he had a double plot, having bought his neighbour's garden some years previously). Both the Sunderlands and Sims had also been offered substantially more than our group for comparatively similar-sized plots.

Wilson Homes made a potentially much higher but unconfirmed offer. Our final meeting with Curtis Mayfield in Marlborough was tense. We knew other neighbours had been given a better deal. The access through our site was not compensated to our satisfaction and Andy almost went ballistic over the value of his house. The values placed on the houses clearly affected the offer on the land, but of course only two of the group were worrying about this.

Ultimately the discussions with Curtis Mayfield broke down. We made the decision to go with Wilson Homes, even though all the details were yet to be completed.

I spoke to all the neighbours to the right of our

house to tell them that we would not be going forward with Curtis Mayfield. Mrs Sunderland was clearly upset with our decision and she did not want to have anything to do with Wilson Homes. Maria Sunderland had been sold a story by Curtis Mayfield about building caveats that were baloney, but it made her feel comfortable. David Sims said little and the Woodmans felt their offer had always been outlandish. They were very happy to go with Wilson Homes and felt Mrs Sunderland would come on board, but none were ever given the chance. Maria's unwelcome and totally illogical behaviour, first in absolute favour of selling then totally against, was more than the developers wished to consider. Developers are accustomed to difficult negotiations and tolerant of many things in the normal course of purchasing land, but constant changing of minds, unachievable caveats and wholly unrealistic land values are ultimately a no-go.

Wilson Homes made a considerably better offer and the matrix was used to assess it, but somehow I could not help thinking I had been too generous on the access and the devaluation of the house meant an effective £50k loss on the land, so our deal was never as good as the others, and this was even more apparent on the day our Land Manager presented to the Wilson Homes Board. First he shaded £50k off the total deal, of which we suffered the most because it came direct off the land value, and which we had the biggest plot. But at 4 o'clock that afternoon it mattered not. Wilson Homes

Board rejected the deal and any interest in the land. It would be many months before a new offer came along that remotely met our expectations.

I had started playing badminton again, a bit late at 57. At first it was only with my old colleague who lived at Hinton Parva, who was the same age as me. Then we joined Swindon Badminton Club in the summer. By the start of the new badminton season I had been selected for the mixed and men's teams. Unfortunately it was only in the third teams, it gave a little boost to the ego and I remember trekking round Swindon with Lorraine trying to find the Polish Club, where I was due to play my first match that evening. No satnav and no knowledge really of the Swindon area. We were thrashed by eight games to one, room for improvement there then.

Some six weeks after the Wilson Homes debacle, Mike Hudson, who had been acting on a contract basis for Wilson Homes but ran his own land search development company, wrote to us to offer a meeting to consider the pursuit of the sale of our land. We were keen to hear what he had to say. One of the questions he posed was what we would accept for the land in the absence of an answer from anyone. I suggested that we engage Mike Hudson to search for a developer (Mike's fee was provided by the developer) and simply test what was available. After all Curtis Mayfield had failed to satisfy anyone and Wilson Homes had made a generous offer but delivered zilch, so it was to difficult to set a value. In truth it would take many months before we could find a developer, and when we did the offer was nowhere near that of Wilson Homes. It also had a sting in the tail whereby we had to pay the Section 106 costs ( a local council tax on the development, ie new road, primary school contribution or even building a primary school when the development was very large. There was also a caveat in terms of accessing drainage from the site whereby we would be liable for excess costs. Coupled together the two elements effectively reduced the potential offer by as much as £110k - far too steep. Limitations on these elements would have to be achieved before it became an acceptable offer.

Lorraine and I both felt that the previous offers had not given us a fair deal. Both concentrated too much on the land for building to the detriment of access and property devaluation. I was determined on this occasion to set a minimum share for us that reflected fairness. I could not rid my memory bank of the fact that initially we had been excluded from the plans of our partners in the sale, moreover previously the access split had been unfairly divided (admittedly I had set the divisions) and finally the large reduction in our house value, oddly not suffered by our neighbours to anywhere near the same impact. This was a real stumbling block for Lorraine and me.

I set these points out in a letter to our neighbours while we were searching for a new developer. There was some huffing and puffing, but in general there were no direct objections made, mostly silence. Silence I know is not acceptance but neither is it rejection. When an offer in total was made our points would be deemed acceptable or not I guessed, dependent on the total pot and individuals' views of their own shares.

I had been at the forefront of all the previous negotiations and dealt with the solicitor on a one-to-one basis during the Wilson Home contract, which was common to all and signed by all. Speaking to Mike Hudson following a written offer from Midas Homes, which simply gave a single value for the site, I set down the conditions on which Lorraine and I would move forward - namely a minimum amount for house and land regardless of Section 106 and drainage costs or access valuation in the total package. Unless our minimum sums were met we would not deal, so there would be no deal. Mike Hudson thanked me for my clarity, and wondered out loud what the others would say, if it would be enough money for them and whether Midas Homes would accept the upper limit I was proposing on their 106 Section/Drainage clause. In response to Mike's thoughts I simply said if Midas would not do so, there was no deal to be had. We would waste much time trying with no chance that I or any of others would say yes.

Mike Hudson was back on the phone within an hour to let me know that Midas Homes had accepted our limitations on the Section 106/Drainage penalties. What was now needed was a way forward on how the pot was split. "Any suggestions?" he said. "Yes" I replied, "I'll email you a breakdown of access values and land values for each neighbour. You will see that this provides Lorraine and me with what we consider a fair share and would gain our acceptance subject to a satisfactory house price and a contract that clearly spells out the limitations on those penalties. Incidentally everyone wants individual contracts this time round, not a biggy. With today's computers, five contracts with minor variations takes a couple of hours."

Mike was silent for a moment. Then he asked how I knew my neighbours would accept this deal, and how we could test it before getting wholesale rejection. My response was short – "We don't Mike, but unless we test the waters we will never know. My assessment of this situation is that everyone is now hooked on selling their land. Two of the couples are into or nearing their seventies with land they don't want and can't manage. One is a builder who could clear his mortgage instantly. Andy and Faith, like us, see an opportunity to make a bit of money not available simply from a house sale. With all those ingredients in the pot, a good brew can be made."

"You know Mike, I am suddenly confident we can make a deal" he said.

"We can but try" I answered. "I'll forward my suggested split of the money which matches our minimum and fairly reflects the land share percentage of each of our five gardens and the final house price offers by Wilson Homes and you and our Midas man can make an offer to each individual couple, as deemed fit." I said it might appear unethical but I needed to know the split simply to verify the total. It was not an issue of trust, but as I was likely to work with the our solicitor on behalf of us all I needed to know the individual amounts.

Three days after sending the suggestions to Mike Hudson, he rang to give me the figures which would be in the offer letters. There were minor variances, which he explained, and with which I had no problems. In fact they increased our own offer by a smidgin, £4k to be precise. You have to remember that all five households had originally received an offer that simply stated the total. Now the amounts were posted individually. Interestingly, no one asked what the others were getting. There was a desire for individual contracts and they knew the total and they knew their own share.

Karl said he could not accept his offer, but did agree that it would be sensible to go ahead and draw up the contracts. All agreed that I should act for them in putting the contracts together with our solicitor. Our solicitor had said he was not prepared to meet individually on the contracts as it would be too costly and time consuming. Midas asked us cheekily if they could use the Wilson Holmes contract as a starter, as it would make things happen quicker because as of yet we had not even got to the planning application stage. We agreed, and Andy and I spent four days rewriting the contract and adding the elements which we wished to include. We then forwarded it direct to the Midas solicitor.

Midas would not move on the money, so Karl's position was clearly a show stopper. The wording in the final offer letter to us individually was also far too ambiguous with regard to the 106/drainage. Karl's offer was £11k less than his original day one offer from Curtis Mayfield, so I could understand why he did not want to accept. In the end we gave him £5k off our land deal and I persuaded the others to cover Karl's liabilities under the Section 106 costs.

The contract took over a month to prepare and as it had a 2year duration after a successful planning application it was a very tiresome and slow process - totally normal however, I understand, in the building industry. I do recall at one point John Hunt, our solicitor, contacting me about a ready reckoner land price matrix that I had talked through with him on the phone in response to the Midas solicitor's suggestion, which meant we would have been twelve months behind current land prices at the point of the contract being delivered, ie our money being paid. John's interpretation of my intention had come out back to front and I had to go through the calculation part by part. John had already sent his version to the Midas solicitor. I recall him saying (he had a good sense of humour) "I'll just wrap a cold wet towel round my head and go and stand in the cupboard while my brain gets a handle on what you've said and tell my mate working for the other side that my client thinks I am a numskull." I laughed and said I looked forward to seeing that translated into legalese.

The purpose of my ready reckoner was to ensure the contract gave us a final day calculation by which our land values could be adjusted, and they could only ever be adjusted upwards. In the event the calculation, which was based on the Halifax annual rolling houses price index, was not very generous to us - it had a pie and a pint impact on the money we received.

The contracts were signed and six weeks later the planning application was heard. We were quite confident, as the North Wilts Planning Officer fully supported the application. Our neighbours had fought quite a campaign and had the local council on their side. So when North Wilts Planning Committee voted unanimously to reject the planning application, the news was devastating. All our dreams were dashed in a second (well, just over an hour). Midas informed us they would be appealing and they were very confident that the appeal would succeed, but of course the same had been said about the application. It would be eight months before the appeal took place and I was to have a crisis of my own during this time.

For several months I had suffered backache and lately stomach pains, and during the latter stages of this problem the discomfort became intense. I succumbed to taking painkillers every four hours. I often had to sit down, and at night lying down caused even greater pain.

I was stupidly still playing badminton, but I did tire very quickly towards the end of games with my stomach and back were frequently painful. The pain during sleep became ever more intense and eventually I was off to the doctor's. I could tell instantly by his reaction that he was very concerned. He said he thought I had an aneurysm.

Unfortunately (or fortunately) I was clueless as to its seriousness. I arrived at the hospital for the scan with no particular worries, but as the doctor went through the scan, I could see my abdominal aorta bouncing across the screen, though I did not realise how much bigger it was than normal. The doctor said there was no point in sending me home – I would require an immediate operation. He also said my GP had done remarkably well to spot it.

Lorraine was crying. The receptionist ordered tea and coffee, we were given a private room and the registrar arrived. Eventually a doctor from A&E came to insert some needles that would allow immediate blood transfusions. I was smoking on average forty cigarettes a day and travelling twice yearly to France and latterly to Belgium to buy thousands of cigarettes at a time. Today I have no cigarettes with me - I am trying to give up the habit - but right then I badly needed a cigarette as it was clear that the operation was no stroll in the park.

When I told the Registrar I needed a cigarette he refused, saying I must not leave the hospital. My response was simple: "You have just told me I could die.

It's four o'clock in the afternoon. Unless the operation is immediate, I am going to have a cigarette. It may be my last, but that's what I am going to do." There was no room for argument.

On leaving the hospital I rang Scott and asked him to buy a packet of ten cigarettes and bring them to the hospital pretty sharply. I believe he was at Swindon College at the time. I scrounged a cigarette from a woman just outside the hospital doors and dragged deeply and with total satisfaction as the nicotine hits my nerve centres. A cigarette has never been appreciated more. When Scott came I took the unopened pack of cigarettes and gave them to the woman who had given me the cigarette.

By now I had gone into a state of numbness. All the children came to see me, including Brian. I ushered them off, still numb, and held my wife tightly, saying "Goodnight". The numbness, shock whatever kept me relatively calm until at about 9.30 the next morning I was collected for theatre. A small pill was slipped under my tongue and I was asleep before we reached the theatre. I underwent a seven-hour operation and remained sedated for some eighteen hours. My son Scott sat with me throughout.

The next ten days were pretty awful. As I came round it was almost like coming back to life, so blank was my mind, and could not move my arms, legs, head - nothing. Then I became aware of violent rumbling noises. I heard Scott's voice telling me not to worry, it was my bowel movements. I must have muttered something or the other, because his words were clearly in response to something I had said, but I had no awareness of saying anything.

On opening my eyes I could see some nurses, the surgeon and another doctor. The surgeon was clearly agitated about my bowel movement, which appeared to me to be rather energetic. The doctor in charge of the intensive care unit appeared much more relaxed about it. The lack of an intensive care unit bed had been the only reason the operation had been delayed until the morning. The doctor was saying to the surgeon that he should not be worried, and with a wobbly voice I said somewhat foolishly that I was always very regular. Lorraine came in, tears falling down her cheeks but a face that spoke of joy. I recall a soft hello before I drifted back to sleep.

The next ten days were awful, thanks to my total dependency on the nursing staff, my inability to have any control over my bowel movement and being unable to make any other kind of movement. This was a complete and new experience, one which still haunts me now and creates an absolute fear of any similar debilitating illness and total fear of any stay in hospital. The evening before my operation a man had fouled the bed, simply because the nurses had not attended him in time. His utter shame was written on his face, no doubt a proud man, an independent man, now beside himself with shame and embarrassment. My dear wife had to clean the bed on one occasion while I was in hospital and I slept with a bed pan for the last five days of my stay, petrified that my calls for the pan would go unheeded. It often took me ten minutes simply to manoeuvre myself on to the pan, I was so weak.

The nurses of course did a great job and the surgeon performed a near-perfect operation, but above all my GP, Dr Anan Vajpey, had been my life saver by virtue of his diagnosis. After all I had only gone to him with back pain and stomach discomfort (the backache I was paying to have treated at Ridgeway Hospital). The hospital doctor who did the scan was gushing with praise for my GP. When I thanked Dr Vajpey some two months after the operation, he was very humble, replying that he was only doing his job and that he was trained to spot such problems. He said that because I was carrying very little weight it was simple for him to spot. He rang my home to ask what was happening to me following my visit to the hospital, to be told by my son, I believe, that I had undergone emergency surgery. He then rang several times to check out how I was doing. Unfortunately Dr Vajpey left my practice just two years after my operation, and today my confidence in the doctors is not the same. My recovery has been dogged with stomach and bowel issues, but I am alive and I have enjoyed a good life since 2005.

Returning to our land sale, the appeal on our planning application eventually went ahead almost six months after the application was heard. The Planning

Inspector was visiting our site to consider the application. Midas, our developers, were not really switched on. The first I knew about it was when Barry Davis rang to say there were people walking up and down his neighbour's garden and to the front of his house, and his neighbour had parked a large lorry just outside his gate, causing significant traffic problems. I walked down to his house and by the time I return to ours there were some ten people mulling round outside our drive, including our immediate neighbours. I recognize the local Planning Officer and asked what was going on, but was taken aback to be told that the appeal application was being reviewed, but the process was being slowed by the absence of a Midas representative and he was reluctant to go ahead without their presence.

Dear Mr Sunderland was shouting "Don't wait, go ahead" - typical of their attitude. I immediately went indoors and rang Mike Hudson. Contact was made with the Inspector and the inspection was delayed until two o'clock. The guy from Midas arrived at our house with twenty minutes to go, with close to zero knowledge of the application, and I had to brief him and walk the site before he joined the Inspector outside our house at exactly two o'clock. Five minutes later the Midas man was back. The objectors wanted to walk around all the gardens. The Midas man said he had told the Inspector it was unlikely that the residents would agree, but he would ask. I said that was no problem if it would help with the appeal, and I would square it with the rest. He missed the last part, so it was only our garden they walked around. Sunderland was shouting, repeating the F word like a Gatling gun and generally being obnoxious throughout the process.

Three weeks later planning permission was granted and I rang the others to meet at our house at 6.30 in the evening to tell them the news (Andy and Faith were away managing a holiday camp). We all sat there and I said "We've got some news to tell you, we have won the lottery".

Viv was first to speak. "I don't think we've met a lottery winner before, congratulations" she said. I replied with a thank you and said "Well in a way we've all won the lottery, we have planning permission."

Viv dashed off to get a bottle of champagne which we all shared with much happiness. I rang Andy and Faith while we sipped the champagne and sipped on into the night. Almost two years would elapse however before the money went into the bank.

During the long wait for the contract to be finally activated, Lorraine had a couple of serious health scares with fibrillation of the heart and a brain tumour. Though benign, it meant major brain surgery. Lorraine was clearly frightened by the thought of surgery but the operation went really well. However Lorraine was disgusted with the hospital facilities and virtually discharged herself two days after the operation. The fibrillation was controlled by a bucket of pills. Occasionally she is out of breath and her heart races, but she manages the problems well with little complaint.

As the time drew nearer to the money being released, Lorraine and I were off house-hunting. My mother-in-law was very worried that we might leave her behind. Though very independent in attitude and daily life, she had also become quite dependent on us and feared a move would leave her separated from us. We assured her we would not leave her behind. I had not had time to return all my own mother's love, kindness and care in her lifetime as I pursued my career and of course as we had moved to Calne. With my mother-in-law however it was quite different. I was retired, she lived very close, often babysat our dogs and frequently agreed with me rather than her daughter – a big bonus that! - and I found it very easy to return her affections. I enjoyed the way she enjoyed being with us.

The house-hunting was not going quite as well as we had hoped. The criteria were relatively simple - try to stay under £350k and avoid having to move mother-in-law or having to have her live with us, much as we loved her. When the process had first started and Wilson Homes were on the block we did find a wonderful place in Cornwall which had an acre and half of land and a granny annex - it would have been perfect. We put in an offer which was accepted, but of course we could not proceed, and by the time we could the house was long gone and values in Cornwall had risen considerably. None of the properties back in Wiltshire had a garden that either I or Lorraine could enjoy. In Wroughton we found a house and garden to suit within our price range, but as you walked into the garden the roar of the M4 motorway almost devoured you.

Then no. 363 Quemerford came on the market. The disadvantages were that it was on the A4 opposite a busy T-junction, a major developer owned the land behind us and the interior was in need of much attention. The advantages: the garden was a perfect size with a clearly-defined vegetable garden, there was a massive garage with a stable block (perfect for one of my retirement wishes, a workshop), oceans of parking for our children and mother-in-law would not even notice we had moved. What was more, it was well within our price range at £310K. After viewing the property we put in an offer matching the asking price. The couple who owned the property were going to New Zealand to live and were emigrating in six weeks. Our offer was matched by another couple, and because the owners were moving so quickly they decided to accept the other couple's offer because they could proceed immediately. We of course had to wait for our developer to close the deal. The estimated time of closure at this stage was March 2006 and the present owners were moving in the January.

With the disappointment of our offer being rejected, both wife and mother-in-law were in tears. We set out on our searches again, but within days of our extended search, I suggest to Lorraine we up our offer to £325k. We posted this with the estate agents and I wrote a note suggesting to the current owners that we would be able to complete early to late March.

Three days later they accepted our offer, but in the event we were unable to complete until July 2006 and had to pay a further £3k calming money to avoid the couple putting the property back on the market. There were many phone calls back and forth to New Zealand between January and July. The previous owners would have had kittens if they had realized that we had removed the kitchen and taken down the wall between kitchen and breakfast room three days ahead of the contracts being exchanged ( we had keys because we were renting the garage at £1k a month to keep the owners happy).

We moved in on the same day Scott moved into 149 Quemerford. Scott, James, Brian and the Trigo boys moved us the 600 yards up the road, with trees being sack-trucked along the pavement and the builders' truck bringing waves of Lorraine's plants. Brian and Scott bounced the cooker as they entered the door and we ended up cooking on the barbecue for most of the summer. We had not moved far, considering I had spent many months searching through the French housing market on the net (even taking French lessons when the possibility of moving there seemed real). And of course the visits to Cornwall had culminated in an offer being made on that fabulous bungalow with one and half acres of land. However neither I or Lorraine have ever regretted the choice we made.

Our deal was not quite like winning the lottery, of course - more like the lower decks of a Premium Bond win. There was one nice touch along the way. As we each owned one half of 243, the cheque should technically have been made out to us both, but Lorraine agreed it could be made out to me, which allowed me to roll into the bank with a cheque in the six figure bracket. The bank manager nearly fell over me as I was invited into his office - I loved that. It seemed a lot of money, but it disappeared very quickly, and to be truthful Lorraine and I have been a bit wasteful. I have spent £40K on cars only to end up with a car that's mighty expensive to run and not really super fun to drive - but there you go. Another £50k has been spent on the house and we gave the children £30k between the six and have helped those out along the way who have needed it, plus one very expensive cruise to the Caribbean. We are not broke as I write, but it is amazing how quickly your money can disappear.

With the house sorted there was much more work than I had anticipated and it took three years to get completed. Surprisingly it already looks a little shabby here and there only five years on, but I have little interest in decorating, being much keener on getting the workshop up and running and properly maintaining the gardens. A splash of paint is the best the house can now look forward to, perhaps a new carpet. There is no doubt that Lorraine will moan now and then, but she has become a bit of a whiz kid on the old computer and makes superb cards for all occasions. She has set up her own website, selling her cards in support of Wiltshire

Air Ambulance, and is massively excited about her first sale on the net. As a business Lorraine would now be in administration, but as a hobby it is near perfect for her.

My first grandchild was born in 2007 and as I write I have three, of course I already had five inherited grand children. Evie is the first from the Boyd gene line, within less than two years her sister Anna is born. In 2012 James and Helen delivered our first grandson, Arthur, while Scott and Phoebe, Phoebe is a very quiet almost shy person but remarkably nice have also entered the reproduction stakes and a further grandchild is expected in 2013. Evie and Anna provide great pleasure to Lorraine and me and a few stories inevitably follow later.

In my day you found a house, then got married and finally had children. Kirstie and James had done this in reverse order, but James was now doing the honourable thing and had proposed, Kirstie accepts and we had a wedding. It was a very proud day for me. My speech was as usual a little below par, but it was great to see my daughter married, and to a decent fellow and they have given me two wonderful grandchildren.

My mother-in-law passed away in her early eighties, and I miss her often. Much of her is still around the garden in the shape of ornaments, trees and bushes she bought for no. 363, and as my vegetable produce matures, my thoughts always return to her. She helped with the beetroot and shallot pickling, preserving the rhubarb, topping and tailing fruit and sterilizing my pots, plus keeping the greenhouse meticulously clean and tidy. During this period we also lost our dogs. My mother-in-law had adored Dray and Charlie, having cared for them from pups. Lorraine and I have had dogs for almost our entire marriage, Rambo being our first red setter/German shepherd cross, a demented dog, then came Smith, a magnificent dog who frequently crept up stairs and eased himself onto to the bed behind me and went to sleep. This would invariably be on a Sunday afternoon after lunch. I was of course already fast asleep, catching up on my weekly rest.

Tramp followed Lorraine's dog. I recall once squeezing Lorraine's arm which made her squawk, and Tramp leapt to her defence, spreading his body across her and showing me his very impressive teeth. I miss the dogs and walking occurs far less now. Talking to the cat is not quite the same. Mind you the dogs never spoke back, but they were always great listeners. The cat on the other hand appears a little dismissive.

Writing about the dogs brings back sad memories of my first dog, Patch, a springer spaniel which had come to us from a farm when I was about ten. Patch was already about two years old and was hyperactive. Whenever he got out he would round up the cows or sheep in the fields behind us. This was to be his undoing. Patch adored all three of us children. I recall one evening we were playing merry hell in the bedroom and Dad came in angrily with the intent of sorting us out. As he moved towards us Patch put himself between us and Dad, baring his teeth and growling menacingly.

Dad backed off and told me to get into my own bedroom and take the bloody dog with me. A couple of months later Patch was sent away because of his continuous rounding up of the farm animals. It broke my heart.

My recollections would be less than complete if I did not recall some of the moments spent with my grandchildren. Brian and Linda's children Grace and Elliott were around five and seven when they returned from France, and before that they had lived in Germany. While we visited them in France, we missed much of their innocent years, making up for it in some part when Brian encouraged Elliott to play football. That provided me with a real opportunity to enjoy Elliott's development.

There will always be one favourite moment which occurred in Elliott's first year in the under sevens Melksham Football Team. I cannot recall who Melksham were playing, but I remember Elliott receiving the ball just inside the opposition's half. It bounced once and Elliott hit it on the volley, The ball soared high, dipped and rattled the back of the opposition net.

Brian was standing beside me. At first the roar of his voice was gentle, but it reached sound barrier levels as he thundered out "That's my boy!" His joy boomed across the football pitch for everyone to hear and everyone turned. It is a moment I shared with Brian and his son, one of those moments you are lucky to be part of.

As for young Grace, it was always good to receive her warm and genuine welcome: "Nice to see you, hello Granddad!" Later when I was ill, I got a fabulous hand-made get well card which read along these lines: "hello Granddad, well really you are too much fun and naughty to be a Granddad". The hand-drawn picture depicted me receiving a yellow card from the referee - a rather nice touch.

Bill's boys Andrew and William stay every summer and so much more time has been spent with them. Much later Emily joined them, but she was not comfortable away from her mum and home. Andrew and William enjoy a Granddad bedtime story. Some are outrageous, perhaps a mite risqué, but I cannot help tell them stories which are on the edge of acceptability. These are after all full-blooded boys. What their dad Bill thinks I know not, but he has never complained to me about any of the content. Laughter abounds and the central figure to the stories as they grow older is a character called "Darren Duck" who has a certain propensity to blow the wind and dump copious amounts of bird muck wherever he goes - and he goes everywhere, the Moon, Mars, cyberspace, birthday parties, jet planes, space rockets, aboard as-yet unimagined spacecraft that would make those in the Star Wars films look positively archaic. His travel is endless, his behaviour just appalling, but Andrew, William and I laugh into the night as his escapades become ever more unbelievable. Sometimes the tears roll down my cheeks as I think ahead to the next line of the story. My laughter is infectious. Andrew and William laugh, not knowing what I am going to say, but anticipating disaster, gigantic dumps and clouds filled with pungent gases from Darren Duck's explosive rear end. The bedtime stories are much to be looked forward to by both the teller and the listeners.

On one occasion I was able to tell Grace, Elliott, William and Andrew a bedtime story with all four staying overnight. Darren Duck had not yet arrived on the scene and in any event the content needed to reflect Grace's presence, without of course reciting nursery rhymes. I elected to tell them a story about a tea party, in truth modified from a story of my own childhood but of course with each grandchild woven into the storyline. I recall even today threads of the content, with the story concluding with Andrew falling from a chandelier and ending up with his head down the toilet and William doing his best to pull him out. Elliott was chased by the cabbage girl, who thought his legs were wonderful, and Grace was shyly asked out on a date by the boy whose tea party it was. Much of it was not part of the original story as I recall, but all enjoyed the hour-long story and it was repeated to their parents the next day.

Of course Andrew & co are growing up and are teenagers now. Brian texted me only yesterday (20th Oct 2012) that Elliott had played right wing for his new football team and scored the first goal - did he cheer as loudly as all those years ago, I wonder? Grace is at college studying to be a beautician and just a few months back she gave her Nan a brush and polish-up, expressing her admiration of her Nan's beauty, a charming and lovely girl. Our next wave of grandchildren, Evie and Anna, have begun to stay overnight, one night to start with and now two. We are frequently exhausted when returning them home on the third day, and whether we will ever get to a week is highly debatable. We are both of course some fifteen years or more older than when the first batch arrived. Of course grandparents' adoration of their grandchildren is a well-known phenomenon and we are no different. I watch Evie and Anna with much pride. Evie's absolute determination to do things on her own is a constant marvel to us, be it unwrapping a sweet that defies opening or operating her latest present, a pump-action water pistol, or using the remote controls. You have to remember as I tell this story that Evie is not yet four, though her memory though is terrific. When I am unable to find straws for drinks at our home Evie promptly announces that she knows where they are. "Follow me Granddad" she says and sure enough there in the drawer are the straws we need. It's the same with the postman, Having been told only once, four weeks later she said "There's your postman, Postman Trevor" without hesitation.

Lorraine and I look on with grandparent wonderment as she struggles to pull the hosepipe across the lawn, and in the next breath blurts out her newly-learnt words, 'hippopotamus' and 'rhinoceros', pronounced with perfection. Is she special? Well we think so. Anna is just turned two as I write, a placid girl for the most part with a desire to keep up with her sister. Just recently when we were looking after them Anna nestled up to me and then bit my chest. It hurt and without thinking I told her very firmly that she was a naughty girl. Her face changed and she said "Granddad!" Hurt was all over her face, in her voice and in her eyes, which began to moisten. Her voice was trembling with shock at my harshness. If I could have sucked the growl from my voice back into my throat I would have done. She really cried, but thankfully she forgave me and five minutes later we were the best of friends again as I hugged her tight.

Anna, forgive me if you are reading this now, but I smile every time we dine together. Today, June 27th 2011, we are enjoying faggots, sausage rolls, new potatoes and carrots from the garden. We are eating late, about 2 pm, as we have been to Whitehall where the grandchildren have enjoyed a couple of hours on the swings, followed by the tractors and finally a short period in the sandpits. Evie has helped prepare lunch, which obviously takes a little longer, but she has pulled and hosed down the carrots and carefully washed the potatoes at the sink. Finally I am ready to dish up. I must be careful to ensure that Evie gets the plate embossed with the princess, or I will be told off by her. Looking down at the plates a feeling that there is too much on Anna's plate momentarily crosses my mine and then passes. Anna is first to finish, marginally ahead of Evie. My wife has a couple of potatoes left and Anna looks across with some longing and says "I'll have those Nanny". She demolishes both potatoes like a JCB. She does have a fabulous appetite. She finishes off with ice cream and chocolate cake.

The wonderment of your grandchildren invokes memories of your own children which have drifted away. At my daughter's wedding, I told the story of changing her nappy, a whole different event to today's Velcro and perfect size fits. Kirstie was just one month old and her mum had gone out for the evening, for the first time since Kirstie's birth. It became apparent to me that a change of nappy was needed. Kirstie could be mildly bad tempered, but as a modern dad I was confident about changing the nappy. I carefully folded the towelling nappy into a kite shape and placed two very large safety pins to one side, then placed the changing mat on the table. Then I put Kirstie onto the changing mat and proceeded to remove the dirty nappy, cleaning her very carefully. Kirstie was already crying, but I knew that if I could get on with it the tears would soon stop.

Eventually I completed the process of fitting the new nappy including attaching the pins, though I had initially stuck one into my finger. Now I held Kirstie up. She was bawling at the top of her voice. In despair I watched the nappy slip ever further down her legs as I placed her on the changing mat. Kirstie was now purple and had stopped crying - and stopped breathing, I rang Mrs P for help. Fifteen minutes later Kirstie's nappy was changed and she was fast asleep, I did master the art within a short while, but not that evening.

As you search your memory and think of the children, the simplest of things are remembered, but often they say much about your children. We were having lunch in the Ring O' Bells at Compton Martin, which had been made very child friendly with lots of toys available. James had been eyeing one of the children opposite. The child was about two, James about three. Suddenly James made a dash for one of the toys, not for himself but for the younger boy, who simply could not reach it. It was a kind moment and a son to be proud of.

Scott of course I fished with often. He loved the woods just as I had done and would spend hours there if he could. I recall his sheer delight when I hung two car tyres from our apple tree. Though in his very early years, the most poignant memory is of course his plea for me not to cry.

I have gone off track again, but as I write of my memories, the time since starting the book has stretched to beyond a year, and of course the grandchildren have stayed many more times overnight. Evie has passed her fourth and fifth birthdays, Anna her third. With each stay more of their character and behaviour is available to see.

Here I would like to record verbatim Evie's response to a couple of situations that have arisen. Lorraine had cause to tell Evie off over her desire to do exactly as she wished and made it clear that she had tried Nanny's patience too far. Evie's response was "This is not my favourite place at the moment and I may not let you pick me up for a stay again". On another occasion her anger was directed towards her dad, who had come to collect her and had ruffled and messed up her dress. Evie at this time simply loved dresses of splendour and now she was angry over her dad's interference. With great indignation she told him "I am not going to speak to you for a hundred years!"

Anna is less precocious, but she is nevertheless just as wickedly entertaining and very proper about toiletry matters, being self-taught in the art of dispensing with nappies. On one occasion Anna asked me to take her to the toilet, telling me she needs a pooh. On arrival half the job was done. Anna, with some urgency, says "Don't touch it Granddad, don't touch it Granddad, and Granddad there's more!" "Oh what a good girl you are" I say. "Yes Granddad just like a big sausage." Anna is after all only two and half at this time but already sleeps through the night without accident, and yes it is my pride and pleasure in my granddaughter that evokes a reference to this basic moment shared in our lives.

My wife now has the inheritance of my grandchildren, just as I have had the inheritance of hers, but I can tell how much she enjoys having Evie and

Anna. Of course it only adds to my pleasure. We are always, as I have said, totally exhausted by the time they go home. They have such energy and such insatiable appetites for learning. My pleasure in their presence is difficult to describe. Every stay brings with it another moment of joy or laughter. Lorraine and I talk about birthday presents and Lorraine says to the girls, "Now your mum does not like Barbie dolls, does she?" Anna joins the conversation with a one liner, "we'll sort it", suggesting any objections on Mum's part will quickly be dealt with. It did make us both laugh. On dropping them home, I always make a hash of reversing into the parking slot and I say to Lorraine "I don't know if I have got this right." Evie interjects, saying with a grin "Mummy says you're a hopeless driver, Granddad."

The memories are moving on and the storylines slowing down. Two days before Lorraine and I celebrated our twenty fifth wedding anniversary, a scan revealed that I had a cancerous tumour in my bladder. We still celebrated with a few days in Dartmouth, though the news was a bit of a dampener. The time together on our own was really nice and our good night embraces a little longer and a little tighter.

The operation to remove the tumour was done just two weeks after our anniversary and there was good news. The tumour was minor and was removed with keyhole surgery, and I required only one chemo session. The first check revealed no return, but the second check left me less positive as a dark patch was present. The

Doctor zeroed my confidence by asking the nurse what she thought. Her response was short and tired: "Perhaps you bruised him when the camera entered".

I had to wait another six months before the next camera investigation, and that identified anomalous spots. The specialist assured me that there was no need for worry as they would be removed by laser treatment (the appointment was one week after my sixty sixth birthday). It was however a further reminder of one's vulnerability. Both my sisters, my mother and my grandmother also suffered from this dreadful disease. My sister Jenn is now extremely ill, having fought off the problem twice.

Jenn has had to live with cancer for fourteen years. It has played such mental tricks across all those years, every ache and pain suspected of being another outbreak. Six months ago, when the third bout of cancer took hold, her health became increasingly worrying, her mental torment cruel and draining. My sister Kate gives untold support, help, strength and care in her remaining time with us. Lorraine and I visit her quite often and there are occasions when I cannot fight back the tears, although I tell her that in five years' time she will look back on this period and think "I beat it". I know it's not true, just hope on my part.

At times we are able to laugh and share a fond memory, on other occasions we put the world to rights, but sometimes conversation is difficult to maintain. Jenn struggles to keep a stiff upper lip, but she does achieve it most of the time; she is brave and fearful all at the same time. On my last visit to see her at home her eyes and skin were turning yellow and as I put my arm out to help her down the step, I sensed how fragile she was. We stopped and I held her for a brief moment. We said nothing and then we walked together with Tony and Lorraine to her gate.

That was Thursday. It's Saturday now and we arrive at the hospital. My sister has been told she has a week, maybe two, to live, and as we enter the ward Simon, her son, is sat at her bedside. My sister's eyes will haunt me for a long while, blank yet filled with the realisation of death and carrying the pain of having just told her only child her time was almost over. We left them together to share their sorrow as privately as is possible in a hospital.

On our return we talked about stupid things, her blue hair, white teeth. I have no strength, can find no inner mettle to support her in these dreadful moments. I give her a long and terribly painful hug, and we both know it is our last contact, we say our goodbyes and I foolishly say "See you soon".

Jenn died a few days later. It was gut wrenching.

I cannot imagine how my sister sustained her strength with the news of her imminent death. She was a mother, wife and sister to the very end, she had no desire to depart and at sixty-one years of age it was far too early. I have left no dates in this passage of my memories. I have no wish to recall the day or date my sister passed away; it is my own way of managing the loss, no calendar to remind me, no day of the month to awaken my pain. My sister's death has been difficult to absorb. I am not for talking or seeking the comfort of conversation about the loss of my sister, but my other sister Kate is in need of constant conversation and I shall talk to her about and of Jenn for as long she needs this help, just as she talked my sister from despair to laughter in every one of her darkest days over many years.

My sister's funeral was held at West Harptree Church, where my grandfather and grandmother are laid to rest. Sadly they have no headstones. The service was conducted by a Catholic Deacon in accordance with my sister's faith. Jenn was exceptionally popular and well known in the locality, and close to four hundred mourners were there to say goodbye. The villagers donated all the food, coffee and wine for the wake. I felt guilty when laughing at the wake and even when meeting old friends like Kenny Mitchell, with whom I played skittles, football and badminton and of course was our immediate neighbour in our childhood. It had been 32 years since I had seen him and it was good to see him.

One of the pallbearers had asked after me. He was Richard Crane, a schoolmate and fellow cross-country runner whom I had not seen in 50 years but instantly recognised. Yet taking any pleasure in seeing them and my cousin Mary from Widnes seemed wrong on this day.

My sister knew her time had come. Most of us

would like to go in our sleep, quick would be fine, to have a stroke and last for years in a cabbage state would be gross. In such circumstances, I am clear that I would like life support to be switched off. Such thoughts are not damaging, but they are a permanent feature of my later life. In my working years ,confrontation, adrenalin surges, impossible challenges and away from work the stripping of a car engine, the rebuilding of a garage wall or the fitting of a complete bathroom seemed almost everyday occurrences. Now my desire for tranquillity, zero hassle and a great game of football, be it at the County Ground or on Sky TV, suits me fine. How life changes down the years. In that same timeline I am also looking forward to my Christmas holiday in Switzerland, building a summerhouse, watching Swindon Town play Aston Villa in the League Cup and enjoying my next Sunday lunch extravaganza with the family. Oh, and very shortly we have the helter-skelter of Evie and Anna to put negative thoughts to the back of my mind.

Lorraine and I have watched the children make their way in the world and we have watched all our grandchildren progress, some now approaching the maturity of working life, all different, and still they keep coming. Lorraine and I hope now to settle gently down in retirement and enjoy our garden and our own hobbies. Lorraine, as I said earlier, has become a bit of whiz on the old computer, and has developed some really great skills with photography enhancement and the making of beautiful cards for birthdays and special occasions. It pleases me no end that she has found a new hobby in place of pottery, which she is no longer physically able to do. She has made many impressive pottery pieces, one of which she displayed at our local Calne Art Exhibition. It was sold the same evening for the handsome sum of two hundred pounds, and this was back in 1998.

My wife is a splendid cook, her speciality being cakes and wonderful puddings, with crumbles that delight everyone's taste buds. I have taken over the more mundane chore of everyday cooking, but I have not ventured into the domain of cake making as I know the competition is too hot. All the children love the cakes and puddings, Joanne, Lorraine's daughter, and Grace, her granddaughter of course, are what you might describe as super fans, though the rest of the family are only millimeters behind. Currently Lorraine is making a wedding cake for James and Helen and delighting in every moment and spending money every second. She has bought so many pillars, I thought momentarily she was building a block of high rise apartments. Helen, my daughter-in-law to be, has a very sharp wit, which I much enjoy.

It has been nine years since I retired and my wife has supported me throughout the last twenty-six years or so, during which time she has had to put up with my many moods, depressive on the one hand, ebullient on the other, close to sheer madness on occasions, but she is always there, a tremendous strength in times of others' weakness.

Finishing work at 55 has meant a need for some genuine hobbies, but in truth these were in place long before my retirement. I have of course enjoyed gardening from a very early age, helping my Granfer Dick or more probably hindering him from about the age of six. Throughout my life I have always been interested in making things, from draught boards as a ten year old to sea chests as a sixty-plus something, in between making a kitchens for Forge House and 243 Quemerford. I have fitted a few bathrooms in retirement, just to keep me out of trouble.

Five years after moving into 363 Quemerford however, my ambition is to create a workshop from the garage section of our outbuilding. The other half was formerly stables for two horses, but today it's home to the swallows, grandchildren's toys and a fair bit of junk. Just recently I have acquired some excellent woodworking machinery and many supporting pieces of gadgetry. It has been like having a super present-filled Christmas stocking and very akin to those years as a child.

John Shepperd, to whom all the equipment and machinery belonged, was once our neighbour at 243. He is a wonderful craftsmen and now in his eighties he has been really pleased to pass on his tools, some of which are more than forty years old, but all are in perfect condition. They have been modified by John and operate superbly. I have told him I will pass them onto my son Scott when I can no longer make use of them.

My wife as usual is very supportive of my goals. It is easy to picture the finished workshop in my mind, but my hope is to provide myself with a very comfortable working environment, producing the odd piece of work, like my recent sea chest. To add to the comfort and extend the usage, I have purchased a hot air blower, enabling me to use the workshop all winter, great news.

One of my other great interests is gardening, in truth vegetable gardening, though I do have some fifty odd bonsai and a horse chestnut, first planted and boxed in 1976, taken from a compost heap at Forge House. Other bonsai have come from Snowdonia, Chippenham woods, the hedgerows of Wiltshire, seedlings dropped in the garden by birds, Westonbirt Arboretum and just a few from small bare-rooted cuttings such as the London Plane and Small-leaved Lime. In truth I do not always care for these as I should and I need to put a bit more time and effort into bringing them up to scratch. The division of our garden works out really well, as Lorraine's interest centres on flowers, shrubs and to a lesser extent ornamental trees. We have the odd native hazel and willow contortas alongside silver birch and a handsome deciduous conifer.

Down the years gardeners develop favourite plants and I am no exception. For me they are potatoes, strawberries and runner beans. From 1977 until 2008, I had a runner bean which produced black seed, the bean being continuously improved over those years primarily by growing different varieties next to it and hoping the bees did their stuff by cross pollination, then keeping the longest and healthiest seeds that retained the black colouring. In 2008 the seed picked up a destructive virus known as halo blight, which once present in the plant is carried in virus form in the actual seed. After 31 years the variety was lost, a great shame. Today I am growing five or six varieties in the hope that bees will again give me a cross pollination that produces my next black bean generation. In 2011 I have succeeded in getting a white seeded bean (White Lady) to cross with a black and red seeded bean (Britannia) that has produced a black seeded bean (I will probably call it Quemerford Black).

Potatoes have also interested me since I was a young lad. Over the years you develop your favorite varieties; mine have changed in recent years but for some 35 years now, I have grown Foremost as my first early and still consider it the finest-tasting new potato you can grow. I have discovered that despite what the gardening experts recommend, you can grow your potatoes just fifteen centimeters apart and with oceans of compost a splash of fish blood and bone and a similar amount of potash. I have done this for the past five years and have found that this régime produces wonderful crops. The advantage of this method is you use less space for the same output and you can grow many more different varieties. Of course every upside has a downside and in a season when there is blight there is zero opportunity to save the potato, due to the close planting.

My interest in the potato has extended to growing almost exotic types, some of which stay red or blue when cooked, others almost yellow - great fun. Today there are some five hundred varieties available, so that will no doubt maintain my interest.

By chance a couple of years ago my son James bumped into his grandmother's neighbour of 30 years plus, Bill, who asked him if I was still into growing potatoes. Back in the mid seventies I planted Mrs P's entire garden with potatoes, harvesting some seven hundredweight (350 kilos). I stored them in Mrs P's garage, only to lose the whole lot to a severe frost, but Bill had obviously remembered my enthusiasm for potato growing.

The third plant that has grabbed my attention is the strawberry, which has provided me with much interest down the years. I must have grown some fifty different varieties with my current favorites being Honeoye, Marsh Mello and Korona. Today I grow them in tubs to save space and make for easier management when they are cropping. In 2013, after a series of failures, my intention is to return to planting them in the ground. Cropping will be more difficult, but I have more time and have suffered too many failures in the last four years.

Over the years the strawberries have provided interest beyond the garden. My aim was and is to grow a perfect strawberry for presentation in the bowl to be eaten whole. Christine, on the other hand, always took the bowl of strawberries, sprinkled sugar on them, then added a splash of cream or the top the milk (no homogenization back then) and proceeded to mash them into a pulp. I always felt sorry for my strawberries. One year she promised a friend of ours, Joyce Small, that we would supply the strawberries for her daughter's wedding. It was quite a headache producing enough at precisely the right time, but we did it.

The most embarrassing moment relating to strawberries came when Lorraine and I entertained her cousin John, his wife and a couple of their friends. Dessert was strawberries and cream. I presented the strawberries whole with the calyx carefully removed from each, and all were suitably impressed. The cream was poured and we began to eat our strawberries. Halfway through dessert we stopped, transfixed by the happenings in the middle of John's bowl. A creature of gigantic proportions was slowly emerging from the centre of his largest strawberry. It turned its head right and left almost as if it was on lookout. We all froze, our spoons in mid air. Now the creature moved from its lookout position to stand fully astride the strawberry. The strawberry rocked under its weight and then the largest earwig I have ever seen jumped from the bowl and ran towards one of the other guests, who jumped up in fear of her life. Our appetite for my splendid strawberries was lost. Today I always cut the strawberries in half to make sure another party-pooping earwig does not join us at the table.

Since moving into 363 much has been done to improve the vegetable garden soil, with barrowload after barrowload of the neighbour's sheep manure and copious amounts of home-made compost. As I dig the garden over in the autumn I enjoy the turning of every spit, and the soil is in fine condition. Afterwards the garden looks like a newly-laid carpet. It's a simple task but much enjoyed - I am easily pleased, you see. In May the garden looks in fine fettle, with every row absolutely straight and the plants spaced perfectly. In fact, I must confess to measuring with a tape to ensure straightness and symmetry throughout the vegetable patch.

Since moving to 363 Quemerford, Lorraine and I spend many a summer's afternoon sitting in the garden, mostly in our arbour, watching the birds. I am always moaning at Lorraine about the money she spends on bird food, but the truth is I enjoy watching them as much as she does. We have a wonderful array of birds; chaffinch, greenfinch, goldfinch and on the rarest of occasions bullfinches, four varieties of tits, green and spotted woodpeckers, an odd pied wagtail, a rare song thrush and an even rarer mistle thrush, fieldfares in the coldest of winters, blackcaps, and then the good old rooks, jackdaws, magpie, woodpigeons, ring doves, starlings, blackbirds, house sparrows, wrens, robins and of course the dreaded sparrow hawk, which visits frequently for a feast of finch. We are also joined by the odd pheasant and early mornings another dreaded visitor, the heron, which occasionally robs me of my goldfish. On a summer's afternoon buzzards can often be seen soaring overhead. In 2012 we have been joined by a pair of mallards which have killed all the dragonfly nymphs and possibly the newts, as well as much else of the pond's wildlife. The problem with all wildlife is that it's wild – it doesn't always match human requirements.

We also have a resident swallow that nests every year in the stables. We train a camera on it, worry and watch until they hatch and fledge. These birds make noisy chatter and perform great aerobatic feats.

Many of our nest boxes are used by great tits and blue tits. It is a joy to watch so many birds and as we sit in the arbour they practically ignore us, going about their feeding with great vigour, secretively hopping in and out of the stables or nest boxes. In late May and early June the fledglings are brought to the feeding trees in large numbers and up goes the feed bill, but there you go.

It is a much quieter life now, but as I sit and reminisce in the arbour I deliberately overdose on nostalgic moments, allowing them to wash across my memory, a bad habit of those in their senior years, some would have you believe. Not so, I argue. For me it is simply fleeting moments of pleasure afforded from my past, or an opportunity to recall the winning of a gold medal and when I hear of the passing of a great footballer or athlete I recall watching them with much pleasure. On other occasions I feel a self-satisfied knowledge that I've done that, been there. Do I miss those adrenalin-pumped years of work? I no longer have the mental steel that coursed through my veins or the endless energy to challenge the improbable, so I do not miss those stress-laden years. In any event I have never thought that working was the best way to spend our short time on earth, and though not a particularly envious person, I have occasionally envied those who have never had to work but yet were able to enjoy the finest things of life. Of course their lives may never have had the riches that have been in mine. Do I miss the people I worked with? A few of them, now and then. I miss the engagement of a challenge, the provocative and deliberate act of winding up an adversary, but such moments are fleeting.

Today such pleasurable moments are replaced by the more leisurely pursuits of gardening, birdwatching and the great spectator sport of football, though I have a mad moment or two at the County Ground where pleasure and relaxation is replaced by absolute anger with the match officials and despair at the end when Swindon Town have lost or played very badly. Energy is still available for making the occasional piece of furniture or knocking up some fancy shelves, a bookcase or a fireplace, or tiling a floor for one of the children. The former is made much easier by the almost finished workshop. Now however I have noticed a more idle attitude to life as each year passes. I still derive energy and pleasure in short bursts from being entertained and looking after those wonderful grandchildren, or a half-decent holiday.

Now it is a December morning at 6.30 am and I am playing hide and seek with Evie, who has found a torch and insists on hiding in the dark and shining the torch so I can find her - not too quickly, not too slowly, just in time to match her retention span. This I usually manage, to be rewarded by Evie's display of pleasure.

In 2011, I had the added pleasure of watching Swindon Town at every home match bar one, with Elliott and Brian. Brian drives us each week, books the tickets, buys the coffees and sometimes takes a pound for the parking. The football is of very decent quality, with Swindon on an unbeaten run. Winter though brings home the age factor, as you sit and freeze through large parts of the game, out of the seat occasionally, clapping often and shouting a few bawdry heckles that soften the chill momentarily, but the chill never diminishes the pleasure of your side winning. Moreover Swindon Town in this same season have qualified for the Johnson's Paint Trophy at Wembley. The day did not unfortunately match expectations, with Swindon Town playing poorly, and the result coloured our view of the Wembley Stadium and all that went with it. However Brian, Elliot and I bought season tickets for 2012/13 season following their promotion to Division 1. Grace, who came to Wembley with us, decided that such dedication is a little too much.

In 2012 we booked three holidays as part of enjoying our retirement together. All were simple and relatively inexpensive coach tours, the first being a weekend trip to Paris, then the Edinburgh Tattoo and finally Christmas in Switzerland. I have to say as I write how lucky we are to be able to afford such holidays, coupled with the wherewithal to pursue our hobbies and a little decadence without worry. We have now visited Paris and much enjoyed it. We met some very nice people, the trip was entertaining, the food often superb and the coach slow and comfortable, a little like retirement.

My other activity and interest in retirement has been cooking, mostly on the savoury side, as the wife is too good when it comes to making puds and superb cakes. I have over the last 10 years produced a family favourite with my home-made pheasant stuffing. Another success was some half-decent finger pasties for Christmas amongst them venison and wood pigeon the latter being shot in the garden and now and then a fine partridge lunch sitting a top roast shallot, peppers and lightly cooked mushrooms and of course our everyday dinners, just to ensure we eat at a regular time in the evening. Left to my dear wife it is entirely possible our evening meals might get forgotten.

In January 2013 I did a recce of my old haunts with Lorraine as photographer, to gather some pictures of my yesteryears. Our first photo stop was Chew Valley Lake, scene of the boat adventure with my brother, then a detour to pick up a photo of the Methodist Church at

Clutton where Lorraine and I were married. Next up was not a photo but a memory of those days when I cycled the eleven miles to work and back as we passed Bickfield Farm ( still owned by Maurice Durban some fifty-one years later – well, his sons probably). There was another good memory as we passed Fisherman's Lodge, a cottage on the outskirts of Ubley. This was where I did weight-lifting four nights a week in my early twenties, with Ian Williamson, who was best man at my marriage to Christine. As we passed it looked as though the garage where we trained has been converted into part of the house.

On down the road a mile or so to Blagdon Lake for a snapshot of the swan's habitat, eerily unchanged in fifty odd years. Now it is a wildlife conservation area. We passed the Bell pub at Ubley (now a private residence) where I played table skittles and first met Christine. As we made our way through the village towards Compton Martin to my sister's house the route took us past a garage, where a spotted flycatcher nested fifty-five years earlier. I recall this because I had to stand on my bike to reach the nest and the bird, as now, was quite rare, a good egg for the collection, and we weren't caught in the act by the house owner.

Now on to take pictures of Compton Martin Wood, a scene of magical pleasure from my childhood. We arrived at Kate's and there opposite her house was the bus shelter behind which we hid and raced our mock cat across the road. On our way out of Compton Martin we passed the duckpond where as a boy in the cold winters of the late fifties and early sixties we played football on the frozen surface and occasionally raced a toboggan across, one riding, six pulling.

On the way home through West Harptree en route to Bishop Sutton and home, I glanced to the right to see Magpie Alley (again the old houses gone), home of my grandparents. There was a flood of warmth from the memories. As we left West Harptree we took a quick look to the left to see if the old pond with its teeming life was still there, but we were past before I could see. It was on this road that I played tennis and football with my brother. This was a wonderfully nostalgic journey of joy for what was no more. It is marvellous when pleasure comes so easily.

The question now as I arrive at the conclusion of my memories is whether I would have changed anything in my life. Well, I can tell you on those long trips to Tadcaster or flights to Edinburgh, or return journeys in a car from Newcastle to Calne, I was England's greatest footballer and the captain of three World Cup winning sides, the first Englishman since Fred Perry to win consecutive Wimbledon singles titles and one of Britain's finest entrepreneurs, to mention just a few of my other lives. How we boys – and men - love to dream. The truth is that my life has been my life. To change it would mean it was not mine. I have laughed, cried and loved, and I sit in the bosom of a large and wonderful family. Why would anyone want to change such riches?

Those boyhood memories for me are magical; running through the Buildings, playing "billy kick the tin" as dark descended, a great game of football, the birth of my first child and those that followed, grandchildren aplenty, married to two wonderful women. Such joy cannot be swapped for anything.

As my story closes another Boyd begins his life. Theodore Michael Ray Boyd was born to Scott and Pheoba on the 11th June 2013. My son enquires as to whether or not I like the name before announcing to the family; a nice touch.

In this, my sixty-seventh year, I have to say that this life has treated me with its ups and downs but nonetheless it is one I have enjoyed. My sincere hope is that somewhere within this story there has been a moment you have enjoyed of Mike Boyd and his life.